FINDING

sanctuary

"In sharing her raw pain and deep sorrow following the tragic loss of her beautiful daughter, Jennifer Hubbard allows you to journey with her to purpose and hope. *Finding Sanctuary* will lift your faith in times of darkness and allow you to see a God who walks side by side with you, a God who loves us all deeply and keeps his promises."

Michele Faehnle
Author of *Divine Mercy for Moms*,
The Friendship Project, and *Pray Fully*

"This book is a miracle. Jennifer Hubbard's *Finding Sanctuary* has risen from the depths of pain as something beautiful to help bring God's love down upon the darkest places and thoughts in our lives. Her witness is a courageous gift and so is this book."

Kathryn Jean Lopez
Senior fellow at National Review Institute

"In *Finding Sanctuary*, Jennifer Hubbard walks us through the gut-wrenchingly tragic loss of her boisterous, animal-loving daughter, Catherine, at Sandy Hook Elementary School. Relating her personal journey as only a grieving mother can, Hubbard shares her climb out of the depths of despair and into God's unlimited mercy and reconciliation, to finding joy in life again. This book will at the same time break your heart and inspire you with its gripping prose and honest storytelling. As a mother who understands the deep grief of losing a child, I could not recommend this book highly enough. Sharing from the rawness of her grief, Hubbard's supplications to God give witness to the reader that there is always a way out of the darkness."

Mary E. Lenaburg
Author of *Be Brave in the Scared*

"Jennifer Hubbard is a woman of great courage, deep wisdom, and genuine vulnerability. I don't know anyone better equipped to teach us how to stand strong in the struggle. Through her moving words and transparent faith, she shows us that peace can meet us in our pain and hope can make its home within our hearts. This book will inspire and encourage all who would welcome a little more peace in their lives."

Rev. Brian R. Mowrey
Lead pastor of Walnut Hill Community Church
Bethel, Connecticut

"Jennifer Hubbard has weathered the sort of loss every mother dreads, yet she has emerged with a faith that's stronger and truer as a result, a faith anchored in the unfailing love of a God who sees past our brave faces to heal our broken hearts. With raw candor straight from a mother's heart, Hubbard offers hard-won wisdom on healing for anyone who has ever loved and lost and dared to keep leaning on Jesus through it all."

Colleen Carroll Campbell
Author of *The Heart of Perfection*

"Jennifer Hubbard's achingly beautiful book takes us to the heart of horror and leads us out to an otherwise unimaginable hope."
From the foreword by **Fr. Peter John Cameron, O.P.**
Founding editor-in-chief of *Magnificat*

FINDING

sanctuary

How the *Wild Work* of *Peace* *Restored* the *Heart* of a *Sandy Hook Mother*

JENNIFER HUBBARD

AVE MARIA PRESS   AVE   Notre Dame, Indiana

Foreword © 2020 by Peter John Cameron, O.P.

Founded in 1865, Ave Maria Press is a ministry of the United States Province of Holy Cross.

www.avemariapress.com

Paperback: ISBN-13 978-1-64680-061-2

E-book: ISBN-13 978-1-64680-062-9

Cover image © halimqdn / Adobe Stock and Ju-Ju / Getty Images.

Cover and text design by Brianna Dombo.

Printed and bound in the United States of America.

Library of Congress Cataloging-in-Publication Data
Names: Hubbard, Jennifer, 1972- author.
Title: Finding sanctuary : how the wild work of peace restored the heart of a Sandy Hook mother / Jennifer Hubbard.
Description: Notre Dame, Indiana : Ave Maria Press, 2021. | Summary: "In this book, Jennifer Hubbard writes about how she rediscovered peace and hope in God following the tragic death of her daughter in the gun violence at Sandy Hook"-- Provided by publisher.
Identifiers: LCCN 2020052789 (print) | LCCN 2020052790 (ebook) | ISBN 9781646800612 (paperback) | ISBN 9781646800629 (ebook)
Subjects: LCSH: Children--Death--Religious aspects--Christianity. | Consolation. | Peace--Religious aspects--Catholic Church. | Sandy Hook Elementary School Massacre, Newtown, Conn., 2012.
Classification: LCC BV4907 .H74 2021 (print) | LCC BV4907 (ebook) | DDC 248.8/66092 [B]--dc23
LC record available at https://lccn.loc.gov/2020052789
LC ebook record available at https://lccn.loc.gov/2020052790

For the One who
makes my feet like the
feet of deer, and enables
me to tread on the heights,
my Little One who
continues to enchant,
my Brave One who
continues to inspire.

contents

foreword

The Sandy Hook School shooting took place on December 14, 2012. In the immediate aftermath, since the school was off limits, for some reason St. Rose of Lima Catholic Church in Newtown, Connecticut, became "ground zero." At the time, I had been a Sunday helper priest at St. Rose for three years. Friends in Connecticut who heard the news that Friday morning sent me texts, and I immediately drove from Yonkers, New York, to the parish. Friday evening, an impromptu Mass was offered at St. Rose with more than a thousand people in attendance. And shortly thereafter we came to learn something of the incomprehensible horror that had transpired.

There are no words.

One month after the massacre, it was time for the children to go back to school. The anxiety this triggered! These first graders were about to discover that some of their teachers were dead . . . and some of their classmates. Many parents were suffering from survivor's guilt. Something needed to be done to aid in the transition.

So St. Rose of Lima Church put together a series of talks for the parents of the children in the religious education program. Jennifer Hubbard, the mother of six-year-old Catherine Violet Hubbard who had been slain, learned of it. And to everyone's shock, Jennifer decided that she wanted to be there and to speak in person to the parents.

This part is hard to write. I had been asked to moderate that session. In preparation, it was my job to telephone Jennifer and work out the details. I had never met Jennifer before. What do you say to a young mother whose little girl has just been murdered? I was terrified to make the call. I confess to actual cowardice as I picked up my cell phone, heart racing, and pressed in the digits. There was ringing on the other end.

Atrocities can bring out the atheist in people; they think, *If there is a God, why did he let this happen?* But that's the reaction of those on the sidelines—of onlookers. Because, as Joseph Ratzinger wrote, for those "who are themselves immersed in the fearful reality, the effect is not infrequently just the opposite: It is precisely then that they discover God."

My friend the late theologian Monsignor Lorenzo Albacete reflected eloquently on the mystery of suffering. His response to the age-old question posed by those suffering—*Why me?*—was this: *Who are they talking to?* For, whether they realize it or not, their question is a prayer. Suffering brings us face-to-face with the fact of God. It forces us either to acknowledge God or to deny him—because suffering is a question that demands an answer. Simone Weil observed, "The contemplation of human misery wrenches us in the direction of God."

However, trying to figure out why there is suffering in the world only provokes further frustration. Paul Claudel pointed out that Jesus did not come to explain away suffering or to remove it; Jesus came to fill it with his presence. The lesson taught to the world by Nazi concentration camp survivor psychiatrist Viktor E. Frankl is the key we need: "Suffering ceases to be suffering at the moment it finds a meaning."

Then what is the meaning of suffering—its value? Suffering plows past the artificial and the superficial and gets to the root of what really matters. Catholic philosopher Louis Lavelle wrote, "Suffering cuts through all the appearances behind which we hide, until it reaches the depths where the living self dwells. Suffering penetrates to the secret of this most intimate life in the soul of a human being." Suffering is the world's greatest reality check. We take seriously the insight of Rainer Maria Rilke: "Things without end are being endured, things without name are being suffered, and this at heart is what we need to experience in order to assess life and its values properly."

In the process, suffering deepens our self-awareness like nothing else, making us more vulnerable, understanding, sensitive, and loving. It enables us to discover dimensions of humanity that would otherwise remain closed to us. Léon Bloy made a celebrated statement on this: "There are places in the heart that do not yet exist; suffering has to enter in for them to come to be." Suffering makes us more human.

And suffering, when it is shared, gives birth to the strongest interpersonal communion possible between people—one that breaks down barriers and effects a profound, permanent bond of transcendence. According to C. S. Lewis, "friendship is born at that moment when one person says to another: 'What! You too? I thought I was the only one.'"

Suffering sets us on a mission. For, as St. John Paul II taught, "suffering is present in the world in order to release love." When confronted with another person's suffering, the only adequate response is *co-suffering* (com-passion). "The extreme greatness of Christianity," says Simone Weil, "lies in the fact that it does not seek a supernatural remedy for suffering but a supernatural use for it." This means that we must not waste the gift of suffering. We need to be able to *suffer well*. This astonishing book shows us how.

The voice that answered my telephone call was bright and engaging. During our conversation, I worked up the courage to ask Jennifer how, after all she had been through, she could possibly consider doing what she was about to do—go to St. Rose and speak to the parents. Here's how Jennifer replied: "There is a presence that is so much better than us, and we have to acknowledge it."

Jennifer Hubbard's achingly beautiful book takes us to the heart of horror and leads us out to an otherwise unimaginable hope. Reading her story, we get why St. Gregory the Great said, "The return to paradise can be accomplished only by way of mourning."

A few months after the shooting, I came across these incredible words in the works of Léon Bloy: "Christians have the comfort of knowing that above all there are *little ones* in the Kingdom, and that the voice of the Innocent who are dead *makes the earth to resound*."

Fr. Peter John Cameron, O.P.

introduction

"In lieu of flowers . . ." is the somewhat expected sentence that rounds out an obituary and honors the life being mourned. They are the words you rarely ponder, that is, until they become ones you have to write. For me, it was writing Catherine's obituary that made me ponder those words.

My six-year-old daughter, Catherine, was one of the first graders lost in the shooting at Sandy Hook Elementary. I cringe as I write the words. This event set into motion a journey I could never have fathomed and a healing I could never have predicted.

Maybe you are reading this thinking, *Nope, healing in a world-shattering moment, such as the death of a child, especially one as public as was Sandy Hook Elementary, is just not possible.* World-shattering moments take so many forms: The mama sitting frozen, unmoving, as well-meaning friends flurry around, cleaning up after the reception that followed the funeral. The man sitting in his car, unwilling to go into the house and tell his wife about the visit to the doctor's office. The lost soul crawling alone into the bed where they were once loved. In the throes of grief and loss, the thoughts are similar, regardless of the town, the time, or the topography. "World shattering" comes in with a fury, sends us tumbling into our own personal crevasse, and leaves us wondering, *How did I get here?* and, *Will my life ever feel normal again?*

LIVING IN
TURBULENT TIMES

The series of events on and following December 14, 2012, changed my life forever and took me through some dark and turbulent waters. And yet I also received the graces I needed to walk through that suffocating darkness and encounter the light of goodness on the other side. What my life would be today had I not lost Catherine is something I ponder at times. Would I have ever learned the hard lesson of choosing to trust when life becomes turbulent? It is not a lesson I wanted to learn—I would give anything to have my daughter back, to see the young woman that fiercely determined and abundantly gentle little girl could have been. However, this is not reality. I can sit right there in that place of want and disappointment that it will never happen, or I can trust there is more. I choose the latter. And so can you.

Life will have turbulence for all of us. "In the world you will have trouble," Jesus promised (Jn 16:33). It's a truth you and I have lived: there are troubles and there are trials. These trials and troubles birth ripples that continue well after their initial crash into the pond. I know this, and you probably know this too. So often we are blindsided by our trials and loss, our pain and grief. "You *will* have trouble." Count on it.

However, trouble is not the only thing we can count upon. We have to keep reading to the end of the verse. Here it is: "In the world you will have trouble, but take courage, *I have conquered the world*" (Jn 16:33; emphasis added).

And here we have it: We will have trouble and we can stand in confidence that the battle is already fought and won. We can be sure of the promise of that peaceable kingdom that God is continually working to bring about, both here and in eternity. It is this promise that makes me wonder why, when the unthinkable touches our lives, we automatically doubt our ability to recover. We accept the failure before we even give ourselves a fighting chance.

People often say to me that they never could have recovered from a loss as tragic and devastating as what I experienced. I understand where they are coming from. Before losing Catherine, I might have said the same thing to someone sharing their own unspeakable sorrow, their life-altering moment, their *it*. On a purely human level, it is impossible to imagine being able to heal from the devastation of kneeling on the frozen earth beside your baby's grave. However, recovery and healing are not only possible but also *promised* for those who offer their sufferings back to the One who suffered for us.

Not everyone takes that path of healing, it is true. For some, the pain and hurt run so deep, they cannot bear to find a way out. For them, self-protection becomes the priority and staying in the safe zone a necessity; life is reduced to staying as far from the guardrail as possible, to avoid any possibility of crashing through it again. And I get it, I really do. It is all so overwhelming and painful; it is all just dark and deafening, and the thought of finding a way out seems so insurmountable that hands clench and arms fly up in the air in defeat.

If this sounds like you—shutting down and turning away from God, clenching your fists in a futile effort to fend off the darkness, I beg you to keep reading. Discover for yourself that the yawning crevasse in front of you is only a small part of the story. In fact, it is really where the story begins. There is so much more. Yes, you will have trials, but you can also find healing, joy, and victory. At the end of that valley of the shadow, you can arrive at that peaceable kingdom. The promise of redemption is also unmistakable: "Consider it all joy, my brothers, when you encounter various trials, for you know that the testing of your faith produces perseverance. And let perseverance be perfect,

so that you may be perfect and complete, lacking in nothing"
(Jas 1:2–4).

Yes, life will be brutal, hard, and dark at times. But if you
trust, you too will find this kingdom of peace if you are willing
to trust in the One who gave everything to restore our broken
world. Because of that sacrifice, we can be confident that we have
everything we need, for it is our heavenly Father's promise, and
our heavenly Father's promises are never broken.

AN INVITATION

As I write this, more than seven years have passed since Catherine died. In the time and space that mark my unthinkable *it*,
I have seen my footing restored in the most unlikely of ways. I
have felt God's gentle hand cup my face and his almighty power
move mountains. I have stumbled and fallen, questioned and
doubted, praised and given thanks. It has been, at times, messy
and raw and, at others, peaceful and still. Through it all, what
I have come to understand is that in each season, my trust has
grown and my heart has transformed into one that is beautifully
raw and susceptible and fiercely strong and courageous.

So, in these moments I invite you, my friend, to come and
sit with me in the unexpected places where graces are afforded,
peace is found, and hearts are transformed. Where in friendship,
embracing grief, authenticity, and vulnerability, hearts are healed
with his soothing balm of love, and our footing can be restored
in places and in ways we never could have fathomed.

My hope is that as we sit together, in some way our heavenly
Father will speak to you, and that—just as I found hope in the
simple and unexpected places—you will find your hope and trust
renewed. Whatever your story may be, I pray you can cling to
the entirety of the promise offered: you will find victory.

CHAPTER 1

a kingdom destroyed: the first week

I picked up the phone, dialed the number, and heard a well-trained voice on the other end of the line: "Thank you for calling Picture People. How may I help you?"

I was unable to speak. The words just wouldn't come. I slid down the dining room wall and sat on the floor, chin resting on my knees.

"Hello?" the voice on the other end of the line broke the silence.

I wanted so desperately to explain why I was calling—the last thing I wanted was to have to call back and explain why we had missed our appointment. In the past twenty-four hours alone I had already grown tired of saying words I will utter for the rest of my life, words to convey to this person I did not know how, in a split second, without any notice, my life had imploded and my family—the ones who had been the intended recipients of this picture—had spent the previous day desperately traversing the East Coast trying to get to me.

I desperately wanted to whisper, "Can you tell me this is not happening? And if you cannot, could you just make it all go away?" Maybe this total stranger had a magic wand and, with a wave, could change all of this so we could all make a mad scramble and arrive at our appointment on time.

I wanted to say, "My baby girl was at the school yesterday. She was one of the reasons for the news splattered across screens." In a few hours that receptionist would read Catherine's name among those of the victims, and if I said what I wanted to say, she would have probably gone home and said to her family that mine was supposed to have their picture taken. But she wouldn't ever have a chance to know Catherine, tell her to smile or tilt her head, or see her light up the room with her giggle.

In the span of twenty-four hours, life had taken a sharp left turn, had barreled through the guardrails, and was now free-falling into a deep crevasse whose bottom was nowhere in sight. And so, I sat there on the floor, clutching the phone and refusing to get up until the Picture People receptionist could assure me it was all a big mistake. "Come on in, even if you're a little late," I wanted her to say to me. "The picture will be perfect."

But that would have been a lie. It would never be "perfect" again.

DECEMBER 14, 2012

It had all started out as every Friday did. We had our routine. It was just the three of us that week: my kids, Freddy and Catherine, and me. We had been occupied with all the busyness that pretty much defined life with a third and first grader. This week had been marked by Catherine's monthly Girl Scout meeting on Thursday. She had excitedly donned her Daisy smock and sat crisscross in the friends' circle, barely able to contain her excitement about the craft staged on the table in the back of the room. They were going to be making snow globes, and she had her sights on the tiny plastic deer that would be tucked under the equally tiny flocked pine tree. When we got home after the meeting, she had proudly placed her snow globe on her desk— the perfect Christmas decoration, she told me while jingling her new boots with excitement. (She had squealed when she first saw that her new bootlaces had small jingle bells on the ends.)

Over breakfast that Friday morning, we talked about the day ahead, excitement building as they realized their dad, "Da," would be home that night. Matt would be making his way across the Atlantic after a weeklong overseas business trip. I made my own mental notes about what I would need to get done even as I felt relieved we would finally all be in the same place. As my little ones chatted, I found myself closing my eyes and thanking God for the life and babies he had given me: beautiful children, a house with rockers on the porch, and a yellow lab lying watch. I was living the proverbial "perfect life."

Even when things got a little messy, I loved our life. Like the night before, we had hustled our way home from Catherine's Girl Scout meeting and gathered at the kitchen island to roll out the dough for our annual gingerbread house. Flour flew as I held my breath, watching the kids maneuver the pizza cutter in what they assured me were straight lines. The banter and their laughter that went from giggle to belly laughing in a split second made for one of the crazy good nights where flour had flown its course and the gingerbread stayed in the oven far too long because I took my time tucking my babies into bed. And the thing is, I didn't worry about a burned gingerbread house. And that was a first. Years before I would have fretted and flopped around the kitchen in an attempt to create the perfect golden hue of a gingerbread house. But on this night, the night before my baby girl died, I just settled into the sofa and called my parents.

My father answered, and he laughed as I told him about the pizza cutter and the flour and the rock-hard walls of the burned gingerbread house—hardly Facebook worthy, I told him, but for the first time in my life, I did not care. The gingerbread house would be perfectly overdone and lopsided—and I was fine with that. And with that, there was a pause where I could almost hear his smile form as he said three simple words: "Good for you." It was as if I had just earned a badge for some life lesson I had just passed.

The next morning I bundled up my babies and sent them off, Catherine with her jingle bell boots and Freddy chomping at the bit to tell his friends that a pizza cutter does more than cut pizza. I sighed heavily, wondering what the teachers would think about the pizza cutter and knowing the weekend would be packed with all that screamed Christmas, which was now less than two weeks away. Top of my priority list: getting the perfect picture of my babies at Picture People. The. All. Important. Picture. It would be the Christmas gift I would wrap for my family, and I had lost sleep over it. I am ashamed to admit—I actually tossed and turned over a 5 x 7 picture. I actually wondered if the picture would be enough because I desperately wanted it to be enough. I wanted this to be the picture that would make someone visiting my family stop in their tracks and actually pick up the frame, captivated by just how beautiful my babies are. I actually struggled with what they should wear and whether they should match. I desperately wanted this gift to express the love and care intended to the recipients.

With the kids shuffling down the road and onto the bus, I now made my way through my morning ritual. As I had always done, I chatted with a phone receiver in the crook of my neck as I made beds, swept floors, and scrubbed counters. When Caller ID interrupted the well-rehearsed dance, I switched over to accept the incoming call. I expected it to be the typical morning check-in from my friend. The panic in her voice instantly told me this was not just the regular "What are you doing today?" call. This was a "There is something and everything terribly wrong" call.

There was no hello, no idle chitchat. All she said was, "You should get to the school." It was all she had to say. Something was terribly wrong.

In a frenzy, I pulled up my jeans and tugged a sweatshirt over my head. "Oh my God, help me," I whispered. I had no idea what had happened, and I went from calm to choppy to scattered all at once and back again, managing only to repeat over and over, "Oh God, help me." Every fiber of my being told me something, and everything, was terribly wrong. I grabbed my purse, backed out of the drive, and made my way to the school.

The children had been taught, in the event of an emergency, to gather at the firehouse that sat at the end of the school's drive. They were proficient at making the short walk every single time there was a fire drill, only today was not a drill. The police cars, fire trucks, and ambulances, lined up like matchbox cars, assured me whatever had happened was furthest from a drill. Just past the firehouse, the drive had been blocked, forcing parents, caregivers, and onlookers to gather in the parking lot. Inside the firehouse, teachers pulled their classes in close. Among the makeshift clusters of students and teachers, I spotted Freddy and his third grade class. I made my way through a mass of trembling children and dropped to my knees when I got to him. Freddy, my strong one, normally squares his shoulders when things get scary, as if to let me know I don't need to worry, that he is not affected.

Today was different. Today he looked petrified. As I bent down face-to-face with my son, his terrified blue eyes pooled as his shaking voice spoke truth to my fears: "Mama, I can't find her." Before the words could close the space between us, I gathered him close and, his heart next to mine, time blurred.

LIVING IN THE MOMENT OF *IT*

Isn't that how it is for any of us who have traversed a path that leads through darkness and pain that is deep and raw? Is there not that unspeakable, inescapable moment that becomes an eternal part of your vocabulary, always cleaving life into "before" and "after"? It's the event you are forced to say over and over again. It is the moment you wish had never occurred and whose memory will never fade because it is a part of your story. Whether you want to acknowledge it or not, *it*, whatever it might be, is the only way when you are telling your story to make "before" or "after" make sense.

It is the moment when life's storm clouds that had been gathering in the distance converge with a force so great they clap a thunderous boom and deliver *its* initiating blow. In that instant, the shock and awe from *its* force bring your world to a grinding halt.

If you really stop and consider when your own *it* happened, you know that split second well—when something in your gut told you, "No, not at all is *it* all right." It is the shift of the eye and hesitation before the doctor delivers the diagnosis or when, after a lifetime of loving, a lover inhales deeply to announce they are leaving, or when a child, now grown, looks into their elderly parent's face and sighs deeply at the blank stare they see. For me, it was when I looked into those pooling blue eyes and heard a shaking voice say, "Mama, I can't find her."

And once it happens, you inhale deep and slow, not sure you remember what to do next because your lungs feel as if they have been filled with pieces of shattered glass. You know the next thing you need to do is exhale, but you can't because you are afraid your lungs will be shredded to bits by the shattered glass that you unwittingly inhaled. I stood there, lungs constricted and not daring to budge. Yet somehow they did. My body forced me to exhale, no matter how much it hurt. It all hurt. It hurt to breathe, hurt to think, hurt to talk, and despite all the hurt, my body performed its most basic functions: I inhaled and I exhaled as I watched, as if an outsider, the flurry of activity performed in slow motion around me.

At some point, the clusters of classes that were forming when I had arrived were organized in the firehouse's bay. The children were lined up, stair-stepped, youngest to oldest, as petrified parents and frantic caregivers arrived. When they found whom they had come for, each of them dropped to their knees to look directly into their child's eyes. Once convinced it was not their imagination, it was their child with whom they had locked eyes, they pulled them close and slowly made their way out.

These were my comrades. I got what they were doing. I knew what they were thinking. I could feel their panic and their need to know the child in front of them was not an illusion. It was just what I had done with my son, my brave one. My experience mirrored theirs until they slid into their car to make a quiet trip home. Not me, nor the other parents from Catherine's class. We just stood there and watched the scene play out, over and over again until the lines dissipated, and the people cleared out, and it became abundantly apparent that Catherine and her classmates would not be lining up.

We saw the fear in the eyes of those who had been in the school, heard whispers that shots had been fired, and nodded in response as responders assured us they were doing everything they could and to hold tight.

And just as somehow the clusters of classes were organized, the line of emergency vehicles turned into a sea of news crews. Helicopters circled and cameras were fixed on the parents leaving with children tucked under their arms. What was happening in the sleepy town of Sandy Hook was unfolding on television screens across the country, and inevitably my cell phone started ringing. Before I could utter a hello, I was frantically asked, "Where are Catherine and Freddy?" "Is it true children have been shot?"

Time slowed to a blur as I assured, "I have Freddy and am waiting for Catherine, and they are doing everything in their power to bring her class to the firehouse." But in all my assurances everything that could be done was being done, all I could think was *Shot?* The darkness of what I somehow knew had happened but dared not utter pressed into my heart.

Someone ushered us—the parents whose children had not made their way down from the school—into a room where long folding tables held a few lonely clipboards. People acted on the simplest of tasks with definitive purpose, handing Freddy and me each a bottle of water as if it was the most important task—ever. They gently directed us to the blank pages on the clipboards, quietly urging us to write the name of the child for whom we were waiting, their grade, and their teacher. Freddy watched my every move and studied my every expression, as if looking for a sign as to how to react to what was unfolding around him. I leaned over and pulled him close to my side as I wrote with my free hand: *Catherine Violet Hubbard, G1*, and her teacher's name, my eyes lingering over her name in disbelief. I put the pen down and pulled Freddy in tighter as we made our way to the line of folding chairs at the far end of the room.

The two of us sat, his head leaning heavily on my arm. Part of me knew instinctively what was about to happen. I called Matt and told him they could not find Catherine. Desperate to be in the room with us, desperate to know in real time what was happening, he called again and again, hoping the answer that time would not be "Still no word." Families and friends, pastors and preachers, firefighters and first responders, filled the room. Folding chairs formed clusters, microcosms of little communities that huddled in, elbows on knees, as the ticking clock moved its hand toward the next update.

And then it happened. The time had come for the hourly update, only this time they asked the room to be cleared of anyone who was not a parent, guardian, spouse, or partner. Freddy was ushered into an adjoining room where he sat with a family friend and local priest.

The governor had arrived and prepared to make the announcement. He inhaled deeply and paused, sending a hush over the room. Then he hung his head as the words spilled out: "There were fatalities. Your loved ones were among them."

The words my heart had been dreading had been spoken into reality. Words so shocking the whole world ground to a screeching halt. *Fatalities? By "loved one," you mean my baby? How could this happen?*

Everything stopped. Stopped moving. Stopped breathing. *Fatality.* My baby girl was a fatality. Catherine was six. How is it that a six-year-old can be considered a fatality?

Faces that had hung onto a thread of hope went dark behind cupped hands and knees buckled and bent as they hit the floor. Devastation—palpable, raw, and primal—filled the space.

All I wanted was to gather Freddy up and do as my comrades had done: go home. I wanted to weave through the mass of people and reporters that had gathered and find my car, buckle him into the back seat, and go home to the house that smelled of burnt gingerbread. I wanted to turn back time to the call that started it all and have a completely different conversation. I wanted to wake up from this horrible nightmare that had suddenly become my life.

And yet there was no escape. I needed to call Matt and tell him Catherine was gone. I needed to find my son and tell him his sister was not coming home. I needed to make my way through the people they had sequestered—the next of kin. I needed my face to be the face that Freddy studied as the word "fatality" was uttered to those waiting on the other side of the sequestered room. I needed to pull him close to my heart—close enough to hear its beating and know that he was safe as the terrifying grief exploded like so many gunshots had all around him.

I often think about that sacred moment, the moment I gathered Freddy into my arms to tell him that his sister had died. That pain-filled room was a holy place; those four walls contained and bore witness to the dignity, humility, and sacredness of that moment. I cannot remember the exact words I told him, only that I knew he would be fine and that we—he and I—would be fine. They were the exact words I had whispered as I rocked him in the NICU eight years before and would be the words I promised again when he learned his dad and I would be getting divorced. But on that cold December day, I gathered him close and assured him: he would be fine, and we would be fine. We sat in the raw vulnerability the moment brought, speaking no words and thinking no thoughts. We sat and we inhaled and we exhaled.

I often think about those few sacred moments and that sacred space. The screeches haunt me; the images of men collapsing to their knees taunt me. The pain, the naked emotion, and the stillness. Yes, a stillness and a peace as I pulled Freddy in and whispered a promise and an assurance, just as I had eight years before, that we would be fine.

PREPARATIONS

When Matt's plane from Europe landed stateside, a police escort met him at the airport and raced him home. Silent blue-and-red lights flashed up the road and announced his arrival. The days following were focused on a single purpose: planning a funeral.

First came the phone calls, so family and friends didn't first hear about Catherine in the news. Then there were choices: her coffin ("That one is beautiful"), the prayer card ("She'd want the one with the lamb"), and the picture for the paper. We all wanted assurances that we had done the right thing during a time when life had gone very, very wrong, and the choices we were making for Catherine's funeral somehow offered those assurances.

With all my strength I focused on the task at hand. Words and more words: the readings tagged with the yellow sticky notes, the family statement we were encouraged to share with the media outlets on standby for an interview, and the obituary I wrote on a flickering computer screen. This last one stumped me: How could I ever find the words to summarize Catherine's life for the world? An obituary for a little girl who was six. It all just seemed surreal.

Then there were her things—all her things scattered around the house: her toys in the corner of the family room, the cup she drank out of just days before—that I'd tell her to put away or threaten to take away if she did not put them away. These things that just days before were a nuisance were now irreplaceable artifacts of a life lived. I pulled her nightgown from the dryer and idly wondered whether I would ever again do an all-pink load of laundry. I sighed heavily as I picked up the riding boots she had left by the door after she had hurriedly kicked them off in an attempt to beat her brother upstairs. Her things froze time, and I wanted that time back. I rubbed the boots' weathered leather and set them aside. They would be among the things delivered to the funeral home, along with her dress and the trunk of stuffed animals we decided she should be buried with.

That trunk. She had been told her collection of stuffed animals needed to fit in the trunk under her bed, as we were convinced it was the only way we could purge the ever-growing and overwhelming collection. She pressed in, smooshed down, and finally, sitting on the trunk's lid, snapped the clasps closed and announced she was finished. And not one was purged. Not a single one. One by one I looked into the eyes of each fuzzy toy, just as Catherine would have, and filled the trunk just as she had done. We asked that the stuffed animals be tucked around her, just as she had done when she went to bed. The trunk, we said, we did not want back. It was just all so surreal.

The television remained off, and the phone rang incessantly. Anybody but me, Freddy, or Matt could answer it. My brother had set up a command center in my dining room to deal with the phone, and in a matter of twenty-four hours my home had become a fortress, guarded by security and a state trooper. I settled into a routine that left me sleepless and vacuuming in the middle of the night.

THE FUNERALS

Within days, we were among those standing in the long lines of wakes and funerals. I would study the pavement and listen to the whispers that questioned how this happened and shared stories about how they knew "the family." We would duck into the doorway of an overflowing church, onlookers in awe of the strong mamas who shared what made her baby's soul beautiful.

The truth woven through each story proclaimed innocence, zest for life, and a passion for the world around them. Each one of the babies lost had lived their life full of love. In so many ways, in that message repeated over and over was instruction for all of us left behind. These babies' legacy was a road map for what we were to do next.

And then, just like that, it was our turn. The church was open for the wake, and for four hours, we stood. We stood across from Catherine's coffin receiving the long line of whispers and shared stories. Friends, family, and former coworkers crisscrossed the country, looked me in the eye, and told me their hearts broke with mine. Strangers, who knew not what to do, hugged me and shared their sorrow. And after the last one in the long and winding line had made their way to us, we sat. I sat in the stillness of the church and the realization that my baby girl was in the coffin across from me.

In what seemed like a blink and a billion minutes, it started all over. The caravan of black Escalades and Suburbans had assembled at the top of our drive. Led by a motorcycle escort, we maneuvered through a town shaken and still to a sea of swollen eyes filling our parish's church pews. My nephews stood among clergy, shoulders squared, having told me yes, of course they would serve at Catherine's Mass. Desperate not to crumble, Catherine's godparents read the readings and her cousins brought up the gifts as Freddy's only request, "Come to the Table," was sung by the choir.

And then it was time. The heavy hearts of everyone in the church swam before me as I stood—with Matt and Freddy tucked in beside me—to share Catherine's story: her fierce determination, gentle grace, and intense love for family and the animals for whom she vowed to care. And when it was over, we exited as if in slow motion to delay going to the place we were going next. I gasped seeing Freddy square his shoulders as he tucked in between the pallbearers, helping to carry his sister's coffin, and I watched out the window, numb, as cars moved off to the side, drivers crossing themselves as we passed. And then we arrived at the place where frozen earth had been broken to receive her.

The reception was held at our house, and people flowed through, commented on Christmas pictures that felt taken from lifetimes ago. A picture with Santa was a nonnegotiable the day after Thanksgiving. No matter how the pictures turned out— whether there were tears, awkward smiles, or beaming faces— we bought them and displayed them in the overly ornate and obnoxiously priced frames. I had always said that one of these years the picture would be so great, it would be our Christmas card. Finally, 2012 was the year, and I eventually sent out that Christmas card.

Just as quickly as they came, the funeral and the reception were over. Dishes were neatly stacked on the counter, a small plate wrapped in the fridge. The security guards who had kept watch during the days, throwing a football with Freddy in the front yard, retreated. Family members made their way home, and I finally reached the bottom of the crevasse.

There were five days until Christmas, and the silence was oppressive. Freddy's eyes were sad and uncomprehending; Matt retreated, simply wanting privacy to process and space to mourn the daughter he adored. And even as the darkness filled our home, I still sensed that life outside had somehow resumed its rhythmic inhale and exhale. How long would it be until I could do the same?

"Hello?"

The voice of the Picture People receptionist jarred me from my reverie. Slowly I lifted the receiver as I sat there on the floor, chin on my knees, and uttered the only words I could muster: "I need to cancel my appointment."

find your sanctuary

The LORD is my shepherd, I shall not want.
    He makes me lie down in green pastures;
he leads me beside still waters;
    he restores my soul.
He leads me in right paths
    for his name's sake.

Even though I walk through the darkest
        valley,
    I fear no evil;
for you are with me;
    your rod and your staff—
    they comfort me.

You prepare a table before me
    in the presence of my enemies;
you anoint my head with oil;
    my cup overflows.
Surely goodness and mercy shall follow me
    all the days of my life,
and I shall dwell in the house of the LORD
    my whole life long.

—Psalm 23, NRSV

1. Consider the things in your life that you think or have thought need be perfect. If they weren't, what would be the repercussion?
2. Ponder the statement "though I am led through the valley of the shadow of death." What has been your valley? Consider the soft and gentle ways you were led.
3. The tragedy at Sandy Hook Elementary tapped into a parent's fear of losing their child. What is it that you most fear?

CHAPTER 2

grace in a lunch box

"Mama. Are you getting up?"

Freddy's question startled me into consciousness, surprised to discover that I had been asleep. It was rare for me to still be sleeping after he had woken up. Especially now. Since Catherine's death, I rarely slept at all, and when I did, the dreams I had dreamt so vividly before had all but vanished.

Truth be told, I had come to dread the nighttime. Alone with my thoughts, nights forced me into a stillness where I couldn't hide behind the tasks I'd insisted I continue to do; I couldn't hide behind a forced smile or squared shoulders. When pain is deep and raw, nights are dark and lonely. Stillness lures out a broken heart and convinces it to reveal itself to a restless soul. And when the body is not yet ready to acknowledge the breadth and depth of the wound it is nursing, the mind steps in and runs the restless and broken soul rampant through the darkness. Nights were brutal.

MORNING MOURNING

Each night passed with aching slowness. At first my eyes would fall on the clock, which seemed frozen in place, and then moved toward the moon as it crept across the sky. From the corner of my room, it would come into my sightline as it moved above the yard's tree line, over the rooflines across the street and finally through the corner window when dawn's light would break through as I curled into myself, reassured that I had made it through another night. Some mornings I would drift off to sleep; others I would debate whether to get out of bed or to stay there, comfortably numb.

It was easy to rationalize: if ever there was a time to just stay in bed, it was now. Staring at the wall for days on end would be something everyone would understand. Maybe if I stayed curled up in this fetal position long enough, the alarm would eventually go off, and I'd wake up in the life I knew and loved "before."

That could happen, right?

No, of course not.

Mourning those morning routines was a whole different level of grief. Before Catherine died, I would lie in bed or putter in the kitchen and listen for the sound of my babies sighing and stretching, tossing and turning, and eventually swinging their legs over the side of their beds. I knew the rhythm of their routine and could offer a play-by-play with the best of the Sunday afternoon football announcers. Freddy was a champion sleeper, waking when the day was already well underway, ready to take on whatever it offered. Catherine, oh my Catherine, loved to sleep and had her own way of easing into the day. I'd hear her stir well before daybreak. She'd start off slowly with a stretch and yawn; then with a "thump" she would rumble toward me with the intensity of African elephants rushing a water hole.

When she arrived at the bedroom door, I would raise the covers and she would tumble under and nestle into my side. I would pull her close, breathing deep her wild scent of sweat and sleep-filled bedhead. She would pull close under her chin whatever toy she had grabbed on her way out of bed, and within minutes, her rhythmic breathing would alert me she had fallen back into a deep sleep. And there we would stay until the sun hit the perfect spot in the sky where its rays could reach through the windows and beckon to me to join the world.

And so, on this day three weeks after Catherine died, when Freddy's question startled me into consciousness, I pried my eyes open and saw he was as confused as I was. It had been a very long time since he had seen me sleep. He stood beside my bed, puzzled, and with an unsettled whisper asked again, "Mama. Are you getting up?"

"Yes, baby. I am getting up," I told him with as much certainty as I could muster.

But I did not want to get up. Every fiber of my being wanted to stay in bed. Every fiber of my being wanted to lift the covers and say, please crawl in like your sister did. And if he acquiesced, I would have pulled the covers over our heads and assured him we could exist in this warm cave forever and the world would never see us, never again hurt us, and never ever hurt him. Every fiber of my being wanted to just pull him in close and never let him go. I had grown comfortable with the routine with which we had settled in the weeks since Catherine died.

THE NEW NORMAL

In less than a month after Catherine's death, our house had settled into a new normal that was gentle and kind. Christmas decorations had somehow been packed away, and the flow of people in and out of our home had dwindled to just the very few who knew us well. The phone's incessant ringing returned to its normal rhythm, and I had grown to accept that—determined as I was to do all I had done before Catherine died—everything just took twice as long: cleaning the house, blow-drying my hair, and folding a load of laundry was each a veritable feat. Even reading just one paragraph of a book I had read one hundred times before left me wondering what just happened.

On the few times I ventured outside my home, it was clear that the whole town was still reeling. People I barely knew who encountered me in public, at the store, or at church did not even try to hide their tears as they shared their helplessness, their sense of not having any idea what to do or say, but their desire to do something, anything, to ease the pain I must be feeling. People showed up at my door to drop off meals with notes saying I was not alone.

Expressions of sympathy came from all over the globe, pouring into our little town. A makeshift collection center was organized to handle the overwhelming outpouring. Boxes labeled *Catherine Hubbard* were filled with letters full of love and heartbreak on every page. *Our hearts are breaking for you* was the clear message. People from places I had never heard of wrote about my baby, that she was beautiful, that she was taken too early, and that I had an angel watching over me. They told me to stay strong, to remember that I was not alone, and to accept as a token of their love whatever they had included in the carefully bundled package.

In these moments I was offered glimpses of authenticity, vulnerability, and love beyond what I had ever experienced. These strangers were manna from heaven, sent from a Father who knew what I most needed at that given moment: gentle gestures that showed me his love in action.

Each time I read through the letters, warmed up meals, and walked away from tender conversations, I always came back to the same thought: Before Catherine died, if it were someone else's baby who had died in such a public act of violence—or even a less visible, private struggle—would I have had the courage to act upon the impulse that was stirred up in my heart? Would I have boldly reached out in love to do for others what was being done for me?

Sadly, the answer I always came back to was, had Catherine not died, probably not. In reality, I didn't follow such charitable impulses when she was alive. We have all watched tragedy unfold across our TV screens and as emergency vehicles come and go next door. I watched other people's tragedies on my screen probably in the same way you watched mine, and I stood at the curb and agreed it was tragic about the family down the street. And I am ashamed to admit, before Catherine died, I did nothing.

The difference for me—and I hope the difference for you, having read this—is that now I understand that a heart stirred is a summons from our Father who is calling us to action. For what we do in love for others will be what restores hope and faith in humanity for them during those dark days. With my heart now stirred up after losing Catherine, I act quickly, and I hope the same is true for you.

And in addition to all that I was given in those four gentle weeks, I also learned much. I learned how to become blind to the stares that landed on me as I walked the aisles of the grocery store and become deaf to the whispers pointing me out as "one of the *families*." My name had somehow changed, and my identity became "one of the them." When the courageous whisperers approached to ask how I was doing, how we were doing, how my son was, I'd smile and offer my well-rehearsed assurance: I was fine, we were OK, and I was confident he would be just fine. They would nod and hug me. I would count the seconds down in my head: Three. Two. One. It was the time it would take for the awkward and uncomfortable encounter to become unbearable. And sometimes, we just don't know what to do with awkward and uncomfortable, so we offer advice and suggestions, an attempt to make a painfully awkward and wholly uncomfortable situation go away. And so the cornucopia of offers boiled down to a single, predictable piece of advice that would ensue.

They had offered to do my shopping, run my errands, and loan us their vacation homes. One even offered to take Freddy: "If only for just a week, so you can have the time and space to do whatever it is that you need to do and get some sleep."

All so I . . . could sleep.

Sleep.

Somehow in the four weeks since Catherine died, I had earned the right to do nothing but stay in bed. They did not know sleep did not come easy, and tossing restlessly in bed seemed a futile exercise in healing a broken spirit and fractured heart. Going to the grocery store and running errands and set-ting a table—even if for a dinner I did not make—gave me pur-pose. Conversely, the thought that my son would be whisked off, even for just a week, paralyzed me. The mere thought of setting a table for two when I just figured out how to gather silverware and plates for three seemed, well, impossible. So I would politely smile, profusely thank them for their offer, and retreat to the comfortable rhythms of home.

Truth be told, staying in bed might work for a bit, but there will come a day when you need to get out of bed. And maybe having the groceries neatly lined up in the fridge or dinner brought to the doorstep for a full year allows the brokenhearted to nap, but eventually the meals end and the refrigerator is no longer magically stocked. Time alone can offer you quiet to stay in bed to sort through a million thoughts. Eventually, though, you have to get out of bed. And make no mistake, getting out of bed—no matter what your *it* might be—is courageous and brave.

So, my friend, I know you may want to just pull up the covers, curl up in a ball, and stay in bed, but I can assure you that, if you do, you will miss the light seeping through the curtains of darkness. I promise you, as hard as it may be to not sleep the days away, to not completely close out the outside world, if you stay open to the world your starving heart will receive the sweet manna from heaven that will sustain you through this desert we are walking. Manna as unassuming as the morning dew and found in your small, daily actions will contain the graces that will sustain you. These graces sustained me while I settled into a life without Catherine. And now what I had grown comfortable with was about to change.

There he stood, his eye pleading that I get out of bed when all I wanted to do was pull him close and the covers up. As much as I wanted to, I did not. I could not. Today was the day he would be going back to school, and he would be doing it alone for the first time since Catherine died.

What was I thinking?! I wondered. We had agreed he'd take the bus with all the other kids. We agreed that he would get on the bus and start school at the temporary location a town away, the same way all the other kids would. It seemed right when we said it originally. But now, on this morning, I wasn't so sure. All I could think was the last time I put my babies on the bus, one did not come home.

The school had been kind and gentle with us when it came to creating a back-to-school plan for Freddy and the other children who had survived the shooting. This was new territory, we were told, and they would follow whatever path we wanted. We were his parents, and we knew our son best. When Freddy was ready to return, he could be brought to school early or late; he could ride the bus or not. Even the question of whether he went to school after the New Year was our decision to make. Whatever we decided, they told us, Freddy would have unfettered access to the school counselor and the therapy dogs.

While we were grateful for the accommodations, we didn't give it a lot of thought or debate. It was all too exhausting. We decided: Freddy would ride the bus on the first day back. When we first made this decision, it felt right. There was a peace in my soul. He had ridden the bus a million times before, and riding the bus with the rest of the kids would give him something predictable in a world that had become far from predictable. What I failed to consider was that riding the bus involved walking to the bus stop, with little rituals and routines rooted to our life with Catherine. And once we made it to the bus, he would get on the bus and would be driven away.

I had not stopped to think about what I would do then, when we would be separated for an entire day—the first time we'd be separated since Catherine died. It would be another "after." And "afters" are not easy.

JUST DO THE NEXT THING

Even though I had swung my legs over the side of the bed and made every motion of rallying for this all-important day, he sensed my reserve, dubious about my *staying* out of bed. It was as much a first for me as it was for him. Nights were hard enough, but now I would be left alone with my thoughts in the daylight. All I could think was, *Now what?*

I found comfort in my cocoon, and the thought that in less than a few hours I would be walking him to the bus stop made my heart stop and my stomach lurch. I had not recognized the storm clouds that would gather in sending Freddy back to school. The thought of not having him to focus my time and attention on sent my world swirling.

I think about that morning often, especially when the fears of what is yet unknown whisper similar doubts today. I have come to understand, in the afters of the *it* that crushes a heart and breaks a spirit, the anxiety is real, and it is normal to believe that this, whatever *this* might be, is about as good as it gets. The thought of exposing the heart to hurt in the instant it is beginning to heal overwhelms. The thought of putting my son on the bus just when I had started to get used to our new routine as a family of three sent my heart racing, and my courage waned. But fear and anxiety are intended to freeze, and we are not called to be stagnant—stagnant waters have the potential to poison.

We are made to press forward on the path that is forged for each one of us. There is a plan, and there is a purpose, and that plan and that purpose understand your fragile heart. Listen: "For I know well the plans I have in mind for *you*—oracle of the LORD—plans for *your* welfare and not for woe, so as to give *you* a future of hope" (Jer 29:11; emphasis added).

You may not believe that there is a plan in a world that clearly can devastate. How can having a baby girl murdered in her own classroom serve a purpose or be accepted as part of some plan? And the answer is, I don't know, but I am not to understand. I am to trust in his word, and his words are not minced: there are plans, and in those plans, I will find hope. I get that it makes no sense, I really do. But this is what I know to be truth: The One who sees my tear-soaked pillow, knows the restless nights responsible for the bags that form below my eyes, and cups my cheek cups yours as well. There is a purpose for me and for you. He promises this for me alone and you alone. And he never breaks his promises—never.

The thing is, the plan may not be what you imagined or even considered as an option. I assure you, it is not some cruel joke intended to disappoint, confuse, or taunt. You see only right now; the plan may be something simple. Right now, the path forward might be found in the gentle rhythm of the life that you already know, and I know that sounds callous when the life you know has been blown up.

I had grown comfortable with the gentle rhythm of life, and that was about to change again. So I know the unrest and the wanting to be done with whatever *it* is you are walking through. I too have looked for a way out and have shaken my fists when the neon lights I wanted to point the way so that I could fast-track through this pain did not appear. I understand, and my heart breaks because I know how much all this hurt hurts. And I also get that it is in this gentle time that a gentle way forward is offered every single day. In those early days, my plan included setting a table, checking off a grocery list, and packing a lunch box. Yes . . . a lunch box. On the day that he looked at me with pleading and confused eyes as I struggled to leave my bed, the sweet manna from heaven was found in a lunch box.

On that morning, I put on my best mom voice and braced myself. "OK, OK, I am up," I said, pointing him toward the shower. I followed the smell of coffee brewing in the kitchen to do what I had done a million times before.

THE LUNCH BOX

I started at the sight of that lunch box sitting there, alone on the counter. It was exactly where I had left it the night before when I set the timer on the coffeepot and readied the kitchen for this very moment. It didn't faze me just ten hours ago, and yet for some reason, seeing the solitary lunch box in the light of day was entirely different.

And isn't that the case for so many things? When we bring what we keep tucked away in the dark into the light, we sometimes gasp. Seeing the lonely lunch box was far worse than realizing I had set the table for four (not three), and then (even worse) calling Catherine to the set table for dinner, as though she had not died.

My stomach lurched and my jaw tightened. Shaking myself a little, I took a deep breath and moved toward the counter. Somehow in the silence of the moment, I found my way. Tears blurred the labels as I pulled the bread and jars out of the cupboard, just as I had done a million times before. As I smeared a piece of bread with peanut butter and jelly. Sandwich, check. Next, the apple.

Tears coursed down my face and joined the water from the faucet as I washed the piece of fruit and put that too in the box. Inhale. Exhale. As I bagged the chips, put them in. Breathed. Simple, as I've done a million times before. The kitchen hummed, the coffee perked, and then came the familiar sound of the shower turning off, the signal to get it together. Freddy would be down soon; he hadn't seen me cry in his three years of first school days, and today would be no exception. Step-by-step, I found my way through that lunch box, but it was not done. I quickly grabbed a pen and a piece of paper and wrote,

> You are brave and you are loved, and I will see you soon.
> XOXO,
> Mama

I put the note on the sandwich and closed the box. And just like that, like a Band-Aid pulled from the healing wound it protected, it was done; his lunch was ready. Sandwich, chips, fruit, and the small note that assured of my love. A lunch box packed and words I had tucked in a million times before took on a whole new meaning. Simple motions done a million times before came back with the familiarity of riding a bike, even though I carried the weight of a million pounds of heartache on my back. And in that moment, my tired and raw heart found its purpose.

Yes, its purpose that day was to pack a lunch box. And while it may not seem much, neither did manna from heaven. And yet it, like the manna, served a purpose, a huge purpose.

FINDING STRENGTH TO RISE

When a heart has been broken, lunch boxes must be packed; shoes, tied; dogs, walked; gardens, weeded; and beds, made. Once you get out of bed, you just need to take the next steps. These small yet mighty things are often overlooked because they are done without much thought, yet they provide purpose and the momentum for what will be the way out of the darkness that finds a broken heart.

That morning, standing alone in the kitchen, I learned something important: Jesus understands the strength it takes to just get out of bed. He does. And I believe he will not leave you standing there, knees locked, wondering, *Now what?* He won't. I believe he knows the heaviness of a broken heart and would never ask for more than we can offer. We call ourselves his, and his yoke is easy; his burden, light (Mt 11:30).

And I believe that when your heart is shattered, curling up in a ball and sleeping your heartbreak away won't help you nearly so much as getting out of bed and doing the one thing in front of you that you know you can do. And when that one thing is done, do the next thing to be done. Look no further than the next thing. Put one foot in front of the other. This is how your soul is fed with purpose—these seemingly simple actions are the manna that will sustain you on what is going to be a long journey.

And so, on the morning that Freddy asked me, "Mama. Are you getting up?" I got up and was fed with the manna from heaven in a found purpose that seemed so simple and yet seemingly impossible. I packed a lunch box and discovered grace inside it. On that morning, he tucked that lunch box into his backpack. And he pulled that backpack square onto his shoulders as we set out to await the yellow chariot that would carry him off to school. We would begin to find rhythm in yet another new normal.

find your sanctuary

So he commanded the clouds above;
    and opened the doors of heaven.
God rained manna upon them for food;
    grain from heaven he gave them.
Man ate of the bread of the angels;
    food he sent in abundance.
                —Psalm 78:23–25

1. "These strangers were manna from heaven, sent from a Father who knew what I most needed at that given moment: gentle gestures that showed me his love in action." Consider when you have offered that manna, or not, in a time of need.
2. "Just do the next thing." Are there things in your life, because they seem daunting, that overwhelm you? Consider what the next thing is.
3. Ponder the seemingly simple ways that our heavenly Father has encouraged you to move forward during a time of pain.

CHAPTER 3

recording the days

I am a journaler. My journals live, dog-eared and dinged up, in a special box I keep under my bed. They record my days, months, and years. Each of my journals has traveled to distant and not-so-distant lands, sometimes tucked into my purse, shoved into my luggage, or sat on the passenger seat of my car. Most of the time, they are part of the stack on the small table where I sit each morning, written in until they are full and then retired to the special box under my bed.

The thought of anyone unwittingly unearthing my box's contents and opening one of the beautiful journals to discover my captured thoughts sends my heart racing as I wonder what on earth they would think if they read pages that I can assure you contain what is furthest from to-dos, gratitudes, and platitudes. My knee-jerk reaction to the thought that these notebooks would be read by anyone but me is to immediately get rid of the box.

Common sense mandates that I march it to the bin at the curb, toss it in, and stand watch until it is dumped into the big green truck that carries away what we cast off. I should probably stand watch to make sure my dog-eared and dinged-up journals are covered safely with the scraps of the week's dinners and dried coffee grinds, and delivered safely to where everything that is tossed away is taken.

But the simple truth is that I will never toss this box in some feeble attempt to avoid embarrassment. That box of beautiful hodgepodge journals is part of me, is what has stood sentry over this racing, aching, and at times unbearably painful journey.

From time to time my eyes fall upon the box, and almost involuntarily, I am drawn back to it. I do what sends my heart racing at the thought of a stranger doing: I fold into an over-stuffed chair, pull my legs under me, crack open the first of what is now a collection of ten journals, gather the remaining nine close, and settle in for what will be a long afternoon. Hours pass as words slowly transform from well-thought-out, carefully crafted script into furious scribbles intent on capturing an idea before it can be lost. I turn the pages until I have turned every last one and reach for the next book in order. By book 3, sentences have no concern for form and drift outside the lines and circle around the margins. By book 6, scripture cited on the pages leads me to open my Bible and discover words underlined and boxes that are paired with comments written and dated in the margins. By this point, I catch myself holding my breath, spellbound by a love story I know all too well, wincing at the heartbreak that awaits on the horizon because I know which prayers are answered and which are not.

The pages reveal a heart slowly cracked open and exposed to the Lord God who is included in the conversation on the page's header. Hour after hour, page after page, desires, disappointments, and joys ebb and flow, and I think, *Could this really have happened?*

And the answer is always the same: *Yes. Yes, it really happened.* On the pages of the hodgepodge collection of journals is my life. My life since Catherine died.

TO THE GOD
I THOUGHT I KNEW

My first journal starts tamely despite the tragedy that drove me to write, with guarded expressions of someone writing to a Lord God I only thought I knew. And yet as time has passed, and one book has moved on to the next, the Lord God of the first book seems very different from the Lord God of what is now the tenth. And I dare to hope that the Lord God of my twentieth will be a completely different one than my Lord God of today—not because he is different but because *I* will be different—changed and transformed.

In the beginning my thoughts were polite, frozen, and almost mechanical. Now I can relay my deepest desires openly and often, voice my greatest disappointments, and even scream in overwhelming joy. There are pages where watermarks give witness to the tears that puddled as I wrote and where the intensity of my writing left gouges in the pages.

And isn't that how it goes? When we invest love in a relationship, it changes us. We just become better. In a lot of ways, we have no choice but to become better versions of our true and authentic selves because we long to show we are changed in an attempt to benefit our other half. In a marriage, in a friendship, as a parent, or as a lover, it is in this selfness sprung from true love that we strive to be better. Because that other person is important to us, we become better.

But I am getting ahead of myself.

I wish I could say I always knew the Lord God I know today, that my first journal is as raw and honest as my tenth, and that I longed to be a better person because of my love for him. Sadly, it would be a lie. It hasn't always been this way. The truth is, it took losing my baby to find my heart.

LIFE BETWEEN THE COVERS

Ironically, my recording of days did not start by purposely choosing and carefully selecting a journal from a large selection. My first journal was a gift for volunteering at my children's school: leather-bound with the school's initials, SRS, embossed in the lower left corner. It had a long leather strap that wrapped around the book multiple times to keep it securely shut. At the time I received it, I thought it was the perfect notebook to record my dreams because then I actually dreamt. So the small leather-bound book became part of a trio, tucked between the book I was reading and the Bible I was struggling to understand in my nightstand drawer.

Then Catherine died and the small journal became the furthest thing from a dream catcher. I'll never forget the day, and I'll never forget the conversation. Soon after Catherine died, one of the grocery store conversations started out like all the others and ended in my offering the obligatory, "I am good, we are OK, and he is going to be just fine." On this day, however, I jokingly added, "And if I could just remember a sentence of what I read, I would go from good to great."

She winced, her gentle eyes flooded with a knowing. "Write it down," she quietly suggested. "Write it all down—everything and anything—because you will not remember any of this. And this is not something you will want to forget."

Not remember a thing. I thought, *Well, isn't that just great.* And that may have been the truth for some people, but we were not some people. I convinced myself and everyone around me I was good, we were OK, and Freddy would be fine.

The truth was, she knew something I had not yet discovered. Her gentle eyes assured me as much.

EMERGENT TRUTHS

I really did think everything was good. I had slid right into another new rhythm and thought, *If this is the rest of my life, I will be all right.* I had learned how to get out of bed and how to send my son to school again. I really did think I had made it to the other side of whatever *this* was and that we had superbly weathered the storm. If you met me then, I would have told you that we had slogged our way through and discovered a miraculous healing. Really and truly, I would have looked you in the eye and shared with confidence that I was stronger and wiser having been through the pain of burying my baby and that the new rhythm in which my life had settled was good.

Every single day, I pulled myself together in the hopes I would impress the watching world. I stood tall and donned a smile that offered a depth of conviction, hoping that the rest of the world would take one look and raise their eyebrows, shake their head, and say, "Wow!"

Even when someone tossed out the soft invitation that it would be OK to not be OK, or threw out the rhetorical, "I'm not sure I could do what you're doing if I went through what you've gone through," I was quick to reassure them that *of course* they could have gotten through it. I wanted it to seem all so doable.

And I wouldn't have been lying on any front. I really did think that I was good, that I had accomplished the task of grieving, and that I had arrived at a place of true peace with Catherine's death. I really did think I would be OK if my life was lived in that season in perpetuity. Maybe for the amount of time that had passed since Catherine died—weeks that were now edging into months—I was good and I had found peace, and maybe I focused on the thought of living in the rhythm that I knew then, because the thought of anything beyond would be far too hard.

And so, my grocery aisle responses matched up perfectly with the words I had started to carefully script into the small leather-bound journal. I was doing as the woman I encountered in the grocery store aisle had suggested: I was simply writing it down. In those days, I would sit on the edge of my bed and pull the trio of books from the drawer.

I would read the devotional and write down the Bible reference in my journal. The pages would start with what I thought the appropriate salutation for a journal entry: "Lord God, . . ."

The words that followed oozed with what I thought "Lord God" wanted to read. I wrote notes on scripture and outlined chapters of the books I was reading. I copied prayers that spoke to my heart and described moments that caused me to pause. When the page did not look as I thought it should or I had crossed through a word, I carefully released it from the binding and started over. There were days my mind would wander, worried with where I would ever find another leather-bound journal so that when they all would eventually be lined up on the bookshelf behind my desk, they would match and be the envy of any author. Funny thing about that time in my life: I was desperate to check all the right boxes so I could claim victory in doing it right—life, grief, journals. You name it; I wanted to do it right.

I thought I was doing it all right. And yet, claiming victory—that wouldn't happen for a while. I had only just begun my quest for peace and healing and had not yet even scratched the surface in feeling the depth of pain I felt in a goodbye I was not yet prepared to offer.

FACING THE SILENCE

Days blurred together as we grew more and more comfortable with our routine, and before we knew it, spring had arrived. Matt was back to work, Freddy was back to school, and I had the day's routine down to a science. Mornings, Freddy and I would make our way to the end of the road and watch for his bus to come. When it peeked over the top of the hill, we would both breathe deep and he would square his shoulders. The doors swung open with a swish, and he'd climb the steps inside. Then, with another swish, the doors would swing shut and he'd be off.

And with that, I'd collect myself and retrace my steps back to the house. It was filled with the sounds of silence—the whir of the dishwasher, clothes tussling in the washing machine, and the hum of emptiness. The morning sun streamed through the window, inviting the dog to circle, sigh, and drop. Sleep for him came so easy.

At some point my trio of books had been retrieved from the bedside table and now occupied public space. I'd gather them up, and with the sleeping dog at my feet, I would spread them in front of me, across the table flooded with sunlight. And there I sat with my Bible, whatever book I had been reading, and the small leather-bound journal whose pages had just about been filled.

I was no longer in a rush to get through the day's verse or skim over the words in an effort to simply say I had done it. You see, when your house goes from four to three, you eventually figure out everything takes twice as long because your body is working twice as hard to heal your broken heart. In this acceptance, gentleness cuts through frantic, and the errands, the chores, and the work to maintain order are not so panicked and rushed. Although life seemed to be moving at a snail's pace, to my amazement there were no catastrophic consequences, and the world didn't come to an end when I failed to vacuum every single day. I was no longer preoccupied with getting it all done because there just wasn't all that much to be done. I had accepted that there would be no planning for Catherine's seventh birthday party, and because there would be no celebration, there was no urgency to get the garden ready. Gardening to just garden did not excite me; in fact, the mere thought exhausted me.

So I sat at the kitchen table.

Sat for hours at, of all places, the kitchen table.

MY HIDING PLACE

Before Catherine died, I would read about the places people ran to when the world exhausted them and their minds needed respite. I would scour the pages and pictures beautifully depicted in magazines and wonder, *Where would be my go-to place? Where would I go when my world fell apart?* I tried to envision the picturesque place I would run to: a silent beach at sunrise, the edge of a cliff overlooking a vast expanse, or a giant boulder surrounded by the rush of a raging river. Never once did I think it would be my kitchen table, when the sun hit the perfect spot in the sky and spilled its rays across the books splayed in front of me.

But there I would sit. Book, Bible, and journal open and expectantly waiting.

I'd read and think about what I had just read. I'd read and watch the flurry of woodland creatures and the birds rustling outside the kitchen window. And at some point, I'd remember I was reading and go back to reading. And as I had grown used to doing, I jotted notes in the leather-bound journal—only now I was not really concerned with my notes being perfect; I just wanted to capture the thought.

I know now that, in the ease and hum of the morning's quiet at the kitchen table, I was meeting the Lord God to whom I'd been dutifully writing. And he was not at all the God I thought he was. I was in the midst of an awakening; I did not realize what was happening. Slowly, gradually, it dawned on me that *he* had become my hiding place as he met me there each morning at the kitchen table.

It came as a total surprise to me, this gentle side of God as an undemanding and loving presence. I had supposed that God wanted me to check all sorts of boxes, to show up at the perfect time and act perfectly in private and especially in public: perfectly appointed with the perfect words and perfect responses. If I met those criteria, I felt, the Lord God would offer a "Well done" or a well-deserved "Wow!" And if neither of these things happened, then maybe I was just not working hard enough or maybe I was just not worthy.

And as we know, the Wow I was first striving for never came. Instead, I lingered in my hiding place at the kitchen table well into the morning. Unrushed and in the quiet hum of stillness, I pondered the stories I was discovering and the characters I was meeting all while watching the scurry of activity outside. And it felt good. For the first time in a long time, *I felt good.*

I think it's a lot like what happens in our human relationships: over time and with time invested, we begin to learn another's heart, and the relationship feels comfortable and good. It is a sweet and tender moment when you want to spend time with that person, getting to know their dreams and desires, being engaged and involved, actively seeking and patiently waiting. That's what was happening to me. In the morning quiet and through my pondering, I was opening my heart to the real Lord God I had been seeking when I reached out and etched his name at the top of each page. Bible in hand, I would discover his heart for me through the characters and stories I met on these pages.

When Moses tells God that he doesn't feel capable (see Exodus 4:1), I nodded my head. And then on the page I would write, "Moses didn't feel capable." I could identify with that.

When Jacob wrestled the angel and gets a new name (see Genesis 32:22–32), I would cheer Jacob on, amazed that he had dared to challenge God. *I sure would like to find the ladder Jacob was shown*, I would think. On the page I would write, "Jacob had a ladder."

I sat at my kitchen table, and I pored over the gospels. And on the pages, I would write, "He calmed the storm, fed the masses with only scraps, and Mary, Mary stood at the foot of the Cross."

And when I got to the place where Peter challenges Jesus to let him step out of the boat and onto the water (see Matthew 14:22–33), I would wonder and write, "Would I have the courage to step out onto the water?"

Unbeknownst to me, I was really encountering the Lord God to whom I had been writing all these many months. Unbeknownst to me, I was praying through the people in these stories, chosen well before my time to be examples to me. And so that's where we, my Lord God and me, met: through days started by journaling at my kitchen table.

A SILENT CROSSROADS

With every relationship, the sweet period of getting to know the other person comes to a crossroads where a choice needs to be made. We can choose to continue on, safe, sweet, and cordial, or we can choose to go deeper. Know, though, that going deeper is not always easy and it requires vulnerability. And yet, I assure you the path of vulnerability leads to a relationship born in authenticity. It is where love, pure and true, embraces the broken, protects the most fragile parts, and dances in delight of every single victory. It is when you yearn to just be better for the other person.

In the second journal of my hodgepodge collection, I now recognize that I had captured this crossroad experience with my Lord God. I had started this small spiral-bound book after running out of pages in my leather-bound journal.

I wasn't too quick to retire the small leather-bound book, of course. It's hard to let go when it took so long to get used to something in the first place. Many a morning I would flip through the pages of my first journal, seeing the same names come up over and over and the one-liner I had written of the takeaway, and I pondered them. And then it happened: one day the words just tumbled out. I couldn't help myself. Peter and the apostles had begged for Jesus to save them from the storm (Lk 8:22–25), and Jacob had fought until the morning dawn, demanding and receiving a blessing from his encounter with God (Gn 32:23–31). And I felt as if I needed to lock arms with these people with whom I had found fellowship, people who had wrestled with God, begged him to acknowledge and save them, and been forever changed. It was just one of those mornings.

And so I took up this second, spiral journal and began to write. I tell you, the words just tumbled out, and before I could stop, they had formed the question on the page.

> Lord God,
> Do you see me? Do you even care?

I still stiffen at how sad I was the day I etched those words. You see, I wanted that ladder of Jacob's, and I wanted Jesus to wake up and to cease the storm that was causing my heart to race. I had been sitting at the kitchen table day after day, reading of all these miraculous healings and sightings, and my heart was yearning for something similar. I wanted some type of confirmation, and

short of the confirmation I wished for, I was beginning to wonder, *Why am I sitting at this table?*

I want to believe I actually asked the question that we have
all at one time asked. And if you haven't said it out loud, I'm sure
you've thought it: *God, are you really here? God, are you really
interested in me?*

Sitting at my table for months, scouring scripture, and reading books that explained what I read in my Bible, I had taken
copious notes, and in my takeaways I had recorded God's promises and prayers, and I wanted more. I needed more. I needed
to know it was not all a single-sided conversation in a relationship of one. I needed to know that I was seen, I had heard the
right words, and there was a Lord God on the other side of the
salutation.

Truth be told, as I wrote bold, I was thinking scared. As soon
as I scribbled the questions, I wanted to take them back, and I
couldn't. Ink had tattooed the page. It's like when you face the
very person who means the world to you and boldly say what's
on your heart, and as soon as those brave and beautiful words
tumble out you inhale sharp and worry the words have changed
everything for the worse, that the words will offend and send the
person you love turning on their heels and leave you looking at
their back as they walk away.

I describe it like this because that is what I expected—
because that had been my experience. I am sure you have your
own idea of what it may be like when the brave and beautiful
words of your heart tumble out. Experiences influence your
decision as to whether you really want to walk down this path
of vulnerability.

And all I can do is ask you sweetly and gently to not be
scared in the bold and beautiful that defines vulnerability with
the Lord God. What you might expect as the outcome of your
boldness because of what you've learned from life experience

and human relationships is not going to happen. The truth of the matter with our Lord God is very different: he wants our vulnerability, craves our vulnerability, as much as we crave his gaze.

And here's why I know this: I expected an explosive response, an immediate teeth-grinding "How dare you even utter such a question?" and "If that's how you feel, you'll pay." What I got was nothing. *Nothing.* The spray of the dishwasher continued to whir and clothes tumbled in the dryer and the dog circled and flopped at my feet. Days turned into weeks, and the "away with you" I kept looking over my shoulder for did not come. I slowly started to exhale in relief that I had dodged the bullet of rejection, and I vowed I would not try that again.

Time at the kitchen table was where I had found some semblance of peace, so to it I returned and so too did I return to the characters and the stories with whom I had locked arms. I pored over their stories and discovered there were not bullets to be dodged and there was no retreating. The widow would not leave the judge alone, and the neighbor would not stop knocking (see Luke 18 and Luke 11), and as if leaving no room for interpretation, Jesus himself locked eyes with his persistent people.

In the quiet mornings at my table, on the pages of my journal I would ask and seek and knock. I wrote the thoughts I was pondering. Only now they were not carved as boldly as when I called his caring for me into question but rather written gently to the Lord God in the salutation and for no other reason than I prayed he would answer me as he answered the ones with whom I locked arms.

Every so often I would offer a gentle reminder to the simple question I really wanted God to answer:

Lord God, do you see me?

I don't mean to make it sound as if my occasional gentle reminder was a peaceful acceptance of not having an answer yet, because it was not. There were days I fell prey to believing the silence was a passive-aggressive no: "No, I do not see you." I thought because the answers I was seeking were not offered in the way I envisioned that I was not seen or, if I was seen, maybe I was not worthy.

I would chastise myself, wondering why on earth I would be answered by the I Am. Me? It was ludicrous to believe that I would be offered that which my heart pondered on the pages of my journal. The thought that the I Am would present a ladder to me as he did Jacob and that I would be deeded rights to toggle between heaven and earth so that I could split time with both my babies . . . What was I thinking? Who was I to request that the Lord God reach his hand out to mine or that he would instantaneously calm the waves battering my boat?

In the silence, I had watched out the window and made assumptions—false assumptions—about the meaning of that silence. Assumptions I will never make again.

AN INVITATION

We stood in the driveway as she pulled off her garden gloves and clapped the dirt from them. She had been helping in a friend's yard. We had met just twenty minutes before, and she had no idea who I was when I asked naïvely, "What do you suggest I plant in full sun at a cemetery?"

If I could have pulled the words back, I would have. In my obsession to figure out what to put at Catherine's grave, I forgot to consider the repercussions of asking a question such as this. And now I had opened my mouth and would have to explain that these would be for Catherine's planters.

I dreaded what the natural next question would be from this new acquaintance: "Who's Catherine?" I wasn't sure that I could explain one more time that my baby had died.

Thankfully, she didn't ask. Before I could shake off the question the same way she clapped off the dirt, she had extended an invitation to come and look at all the plants that would work. And before I had a chance to consider the invitation, I said, "Sure, that would be great."

The next day we walked the rows, looking at the plants that had finally come out from under cover of the greenhouses. She urged me to pull the ones I liked into the aisle and then asked me, "Which do you think Catherine would have chosen?" And so those that I was sure Catherine would have loved joined the ones I had picked. Then she smiled and asked, "Are there any others that look like Catherine? Pull those too."

To this question, I pulled the plants that were whimsical and graceful. We walked the aisles, pulled pots we liked, and she asked me about Catherine—the very first time I had been asked about her casually since she died. She asked what she loved and what she was like, and when we had walked every row and had pulled everything we could pull, she looked at me. Tears had been streaming unabashedly down her face, and she said, "I wish I could have met her." And then, catching herself, she tilted her head and gasped, "I am so sorry." Having said what was on her heart, she inhaled, shook her head, and looked at the plants we had assembled for the planter at Catherine's grave.

And then it happened, like the knowing, gentle eyes of the woman in the grocery store who had advised me to "write it down, write it all down—everything and anything," my new-found friend's eyes spoke a similar truth. We stood looking at what would become the planter, and she said to no one in particular, "This really needs Jacob's ladder."

Her eyes caught mine as she whispered, "Jacob's ladder is what this needs. Have you ever seen Jacob's ladder?" And I just knew. I. Just. Knew. And when I got home, I wrote it down. I wrote down the day. And with tears now streaming down my face, I wrote:

> Lord God,
> The ladder . . . you know.

HE SEES YOU

It was from my new, green-thumbed friend that I received the confirmation I so badly needed in the least likely of places: a plant nursery I had no idea existed or that I would have been walking through otherwise. In this unexpected place and time I was afforded the reassurance that "no, it is not all for nothing" and "yes, my child, I see you."

All of it—sitting on my bedside and lingering over the words I had written in the quiet of the morning or wrestling with their very essence—brought me to that very place where my heart was cracked open for the very first time, and I felt that my prayers had been heard and answered.

I discovered—and one day you likely will too—that these answers don't always come in the shape and form we want. We may not like the answer and we may balk; we may even walk away because the timing is not what we want it to be. Believe me, every single utterance you make to God is not for nothing—nothing is wasted. Because, my friends, that ongoing conversation is more than a conversation; it is prayer. And we are promised, when we pray with a heart seeking, longing, and true, that he will hear, he will listen, *and he will respond.*

Sometimes I have forgotten that last part. So, I will write it down here:

> He will respond.
> He will respond in his time.

My journals are this reminder for me. And so, while I still cringe thinking someone could someday mistakenly unearth and read the journals under my bed, I will not toss them to the curb—not now, and I pray not ever—because on the pages are my life and a living witness that the Lord God does answer prayers, calm the storm, and provide the space and time to ascend and descend the ladder I desperately need.

One day when Freddy reads the pages of my hodgepodge collection, he will encounter pages where my writing is tentative and shy to admit the longings of my heart and pages carefully thought out and beautifully crafted to sing them out loud. He will find pages that may reveal a moment when my thoughts aligned with scripture and words spilled from the pages of my journals into the margins of my Bible. And he will see the moment when I faced a storm that I thought would crush me. I pray that what he knows and what he does with the knowledge becomes a vibrant dialogue that erupts in his life.

Until then, the collection serves as my reminder—now and in the future. I am still writing each day, and there will still be days when I will settle into a comfortable chair and pore over the pages and read the prayers I dared utter, longing for what my heart longed for and seeking what my soul sought. I will be reminded of how questions with which I wrestled were presented raw and bold and how graces afforded were received with gratitude soft and tender.

And like the journey I have walked the past seven years, I will know that the much-covered territory is transforming me into who I will be, ready for whatever awaits on the horizon. And as I did then, I do now: I write it all down. I write down the days in eager anticipation of what they will one day reveal. Because they will reveal so much. Oh, my friend, there is so much more.

find your sanctuary

> Ask and it will be given to you; seek and you will find; knock and the door will be opened to you. For everyone who asks, receives; the one who seeks, finds; and to the one who knocks, the door will be opened.
>
> —Matthew 7:7–8

1. Do you journal? Consider your journals and how you write. What does your journal say about your relationship with the Lord?
2. If you keep a journal, go back and read from an earlier time of your life. What would you now say to that person you were then? (If you don't keep a journal, consider starting one!)
3. "Believe me, every single utterance you make to God is not for nothing—nothing is wasted. Because that ongoing conversation is more than a conversation; it is prayer." For what are you praying with an earnest heart? What are you seeking?

CHAPTER 4

peace beyond the breakers

I prayed for a check box. Yes, you read that correctly. I prayed for a check box, a box I could either darken completely or mark with a big, bold X to guarantee that I would be spared any future heartbreak. Storms would stay at bay because they would know I had endured pain plenty enough for a lifetime.

It seemed things should have been getting better, but they were getting worse, and I felt if I were going to maintain my composure, continue to face forward and be the Lord God's good and faithful servant, the storms needed to stop. I thought I was entitled to a break. I felt I had earned the right to check the pain and trials box and be spared whatever heartbreak was building in the clouds that gathered and were darkening on the horizon. I had checked the box before Catherine died, checked it again when she was killed, and here I was still checking all sorts of suffering boxes. Yet I felt as if the harder I prayed for the check box, the worse things got.

As much as I would very much like suffering to be a one-and-done proposition, it's not. I should have known this. The book of James warns us: we will encounter trials—many trials—and when we do, we should consider it a blessing: "Consider it all joy, my brothers, when you encounter various trials, for you know that the testing of your faith produces perseverance. And let perseverance be perfect, so that you may be perfect and complete, lacking in nothing" (Jas 1:2–4).

Count it all joy. Lacking nothing. I will face trials—and I am supposed to consider them all a blessing. Really?

That last part was tough. I understand that this is not heaven: there will be trials, there will be pain, and there will be tension. But what about when the storms just don't stop? What happens when, having just walked through a season of trials, pain, and tension, the storm clouds gather again on the horizon? What happens when the ground hasn't even yet dried from the storm's pelting rain before another gale descends? Then what?

Well, for me, at times I just want to throw my arms up in the air and scream, "Enough!" Hardly a joyful—and clearly not a "feeling blessed"—response.

Maybe you get what I am saying. When the storms don't stop, the pain settles into knees that have pressed relentlessly into the wooden planks of floors and pews as you've begged for respite that doesn't come, making you question whether your pleas are falling on deaf ears or if there are even ears out there. The pressure builds and stretches until you hit a breaking point, and then you collapse.

My beautiful friend, I get it. When the storms don't stop and you are pushed, what you encounter is raw and sometimes ugly. And sometimes it just needs to get raw and ugly so you can name the storm.

SEEING THE STORM
CLOUDS GATHER

I had defined *good* as not fighting an internal wrestling match just to get out of bed every day and *peace* as the time I spent at my kitchen table. My family and I were OK maneuvering through life in our individual silos, processing losing Catherine in our own ways.

I had managed to convince myself and everyone around me that I was good. The silence that settled over my marriage was chalked up to grieving our unique loss in ways that made sense for each of us, and Freddy would soon take to the ball field. Baseball would be a normal he knew and could count on. So, by my definition, I was good, we were OK, and Freddy was, in fact, doing fine. I thought if I said it enough, it would be truth that would settle into my heart and shush the whispers that had started to tell me otherwise.

And yet convincing myself, as I would come to realize, only got me so far. The reality is, before I could say I was truly OK, I would have to realize I was not.

That simple reality of realizing I was not OK caused a huge problem. I thought speaking my disappointments, my sorrow, and my fear to my Lord God would make me an ingrate. I thought if I looked less than happy, peaceful, and completely surrendered to his will, I would be a farce of little faith. I really did think I just needed to gratefully accept whatever came my way because it was from God: no back talk, no questioning, just acceptance.

My big idea was to ignore the emotions that were bubbling up and hope that either they would go away or I would grow to just accept them. Our life had become somewhat quiet, and we were all faced forward. I did not want to make something out of what I thought I should just get over.

Ignoring the storms that were brewing in my heart was like ignoring the breakwaters churning up in the distance.

WATCH THE BREAKWATERS

Have you ever watched a storm brewing on the horizon? A storm leaves no room to question what is coming, no opportunity to rein in the gathering force; undeniable and irresistible, it cannot be ignored.

My father and I used to sit beside the ocean and watch the storms form across the waves. He would always comment about the wall of water that was rushing defiantly toward us and how nothing was going to get in its way. As the storm intensified, the waters would shift, and I could feel the air change right about the same time. "Watch the breakwaters," he would tell me. He was fascinated with their intensity. Mesmerized by the barrier they created, he'd tell me the breakwaters eased the blow of the ocean's tides rolling in and should not be underestimated. But, he told me, they also fooled; they were a curious creature that sometimes needed to be faced down because, when they were faced, the rolling waters that lay beyond were like nothing else on this earth.

It wasn't until I had children that I fully understood what my father had explained so many years before. During the annual summer vacation I would take with my kids, we would go "out the cut" where we would face the breakwaters head-on. We would answer the call to the ocean's deep, rolling waters. It would be a full day that required planning and packing and bracing. Catherine and I would clench our jaws when we rounded the corner and saw the breakwaters warning us to come no closer. Without fail, I would hear my father's voice rattle through my head. "The breakwaters are a curious creature and not to be reckoned with by just anyone."

Catherine would sit in my lap, and with her legs stretched over mine, she would keep her chin tucked into the top of her life vest as we made our way out over the water in a boat. The menacing breakers would do everything to convince us to turn around and return to the safe harbors and the shore. When we didn't acquiesce and continued on our mission, they would spit and hiss as the water became progressively choppy. Freddy loved it. He'd lean into the situation and embrace the adventure— the choppier, the better. Catherine and I kept our heads tucked down, bracing each time the stern slammed down. I was sure we would capsize and be labeled "victims of the breakers."

The waves crashed and the stern slammed and I'd urge, "Let's just go back," but we would continue full speed. Just about when I thought the assault would never end, it would suddenly stop. Catherine and I would lift our heads, and instinctively she would lift her right hand to my cheek. She'd lean back, our eyes would meet, and we would smile in a knowing way: we had made it.

We had done it. We had broken through the breakers and were welcomed into the rolling waters of the ocean's depths.

THE BOXES

Emotions, like breakers, can't just be ignored; sometimes you just have to hold on and power through.

I did not acknowledge right at the outset the ripples of emotion and other effects Catherine's death had on me, Matt, and Freddy. My "dealing with it" was treating the whole thing as something I just needed to accept. And yet my emotions were gaining momentum and force, forming waves I hadn't anticipated that eventually crashed over me. Maybe I should have been alert and hypersensitive to the storm brewing on the horizon. Maybe I should have called what was happening in my life for what it was.

I really wanted a break from the pain and hurt and all that life seemed to be throwing at me. When I lingered at my kitchen table, God's word emerged, yet I felt I was wasting time not doing what I really should have been doing. At times, the stress of keeping it all together, of being everything to everyone, felt like when I was a little girl and I would taunt the waves my father warned me about.

Inevitably, one would pull me under, and I'd end up flailing my arms, kicking my legs, and sucking in what felt like gallons of saltwater. When my feet eventually found bottom, I would push up and break through the surface, gasping for air, hair stuck to my face and bathing suit full of sand. Quick to want to recover and having newfound footing, I'd spit out the saltwater, dunk under the water to smooth out my hair and empty the sand from my swimsuit, and go right back to taunting the waves.

On the days when I most needed a break, I would think, *If I could only find the bottom, I could push off, spit, straighten, and empty the sand.* This approach worked for a while . . . until the evidence boxes arrived.

I hardly knew what to make of them, sitting there on the table. I wasn't even there when they arrived. All I know is that they sat on the dining room table, her name staring at me.

> Catherine Hubbard 1 of 2
> Catherine Hubbard 2 of 2

We had come so far. But now, items that were sent to school with so much excitement and hope in September stared at me, offering nothing but angst and anxiety. *Not this . . .*

We had made it through the second half of the school year and all that was left were the awkward and clunky year-end celebrations—the rites and rituals that assured the students that they had finished the school year well and were ready to move on to the next grade. The highlight of which was the Author's Tea.

THE AUTHOR'S TEA

The Author's Tea—a tradition since kindergarten—involved listening as my son read one of his writing samples to his classmates and their parents. I had arrived at the event a little early and looked around the room, and the thought came to me that grief does not discriminate based on age, race, or profession. Parents and children, teachers and administrators, young and old—everyone looked exhausted and threadbare. I am not sure anyone really wanted to be there. But we all exchanged niceties, and I took up my usual mantra: I was good, we were OK, and Freddy would be fine. All of us smiled as each child read what they had chosen because that's what we parents do: we smile, we encourage, and we urge the little souls in our care to move forward no matter how scary it may be.

When finally it was Freddy's turn, he took his place on the stool in the center of the semicircle, cleared his throat, and started reading. His choice was innately sweet. He read each page confidently, showing the illustration after each page was read. Then he added, at long last, "The End."

Yes! He was done, and in a couple of days it would be summer. We could check this box called third grade and move on.

But wait. He turned the page, and I realized *he wasn't done*. There was one more page. Just as all the others had done, he started reading the author's biography.

"My name is Freddy Hubbard. I have a mom, a dad, and a sister." He stopped and looked up at me. It felt as if the whole room stopped and looked at me. They all knew what had happened to his sister. He paused, questioning, trying to read my expression to know what he should do next. He had chosen something he had written when Catherine was alive, and now she wasn't. So what did that mean? Did he still have a sister? And did he have to tell people he *had* a sister because he really didn't want to get into it. It was all so confusing for an eight-year-old.

His big eyes pleaded for the answer as to what to do. He was so close to finishing, so close to closing this chapter of his life. I wanted to go up to him and kneel in front of the stool. Nose to nose I wanted to do what I had done so many times before and cup his face and whisper without blinking or shifting my gaze, "You got this. And if you give up now, you will regret it. You got this, and I got you." But that would have been a complete embarrassment for my son and I knew it, so I didn't do it. I just sat there and nodded ever so slightly.

I didn't realize what was coming next because, if I had, I probably would have pushed back from my place in the semicircle, shook my head, and in a tone that meant it, said, "Let's call it, Freddy. Just close the book, and let's go." I would have gathered him in as I wanted to do at the firehouse and said, *Let's go home.*

But instead, I nodded and smiled with the look that parents give their children that says, "You are good, keep going."

His eyes seemed to get a little wider as if he could not believe what I was asking him to do, but he squared his shoulders and began again: ". . . a sister and a dog named Sammy."

Sammy Girl. I didn't even think that he would have included her.

Sammy was our too-many-years-old-to-remember yellow lab, who had been living with the aches, pains, and ailments age brings. Before Catherine died we had realized that the aches and pains she was experiencing were too much to ask her to carry, and we needed to let her go. We decided, though, to wait to say goodbye until after Christmas. We wanted to be able to help Freddy and Catherine navigate what we thought would be their first experience of grief without the added layer of going to school.

But two weeks after Catherine died, Sammy Girl's condition grew worse and there was no way around it: it was clear we needed to say goodbye to Sammy. Matt had made the appointment with the veterinarian, and I told Freddy that Sammy wouldn't be coming home so if he wanted to tell her anything, now would be a good time. He leaned off the couch to where she was lying on the floor in front of him. Looking down the bridge of her nose, he whispered, "Tell her I said hi."

And there at the Author's Tea the whole thing was coming full circle, in full view of his classmates and their parents. With "a dog named Sammy," he finished and closed the book. He had done what he needed to do and could say he finished strong. My heart ached for him, and I was exhausted, but it was done. A small reception ensued, a clipboard was passed, and children who would be going home with their parents were dismissed. Freddy did as he had done every day that spring; he opted to take the bus. I realize now that, in a world that had become completely unpredictable, he had found predictable. Taking the bus home—it was predictable. Under the guise of beating the bus, I quickly thanked his teacher, unsure if I could hold back my tears until I could collapse into the front seat of the car. Only then, on my way home, did I allow the weeping to come. In those days I cried a lot in the car.

All of it just seemed too much. I was tired of crying, I was tired of watching my boy square his shoulders, and I was tired of pretending everything was all right. I needed a break and he needed a break, and I was convinced summer would be just that for both of us. We would sleep in, no obligations, no schedule— nothing but tackling each day as it came. We wouldn't even travel to the places we had traveled every summer since he was born. As hard a decision as that was, I felt a glimmer of peace knowing we would float through the next three expectation-free months.

When I arrived back at home, I found the two boxes waiting for me. Two boxes with her name staring at me, taunting. Taunting me in the same way the breakwaters once had.

THE BREAKING

The boxes of Catherine's belongings, culled from the aftermath of the shooting, stayed in the dining room. I did not know what to make of them—in the same way I did not know what to make of my baby girl being labeled a "fatality." I would work around them and move them to different corners, as if that would change anything. The storm was brewing, the winds were shifting, and my eyes were on the breakers and the wall of water marching toward me, arriving at the light by the Stop and Shop. It was the dead of night, I was tired, and the waves hissed and spit as I thought about the simple fact that I needed groceries.

There were weeks when shopping during the day was just too much. Some days I just didn't want to see people, felt too tired to carry a conversation. I didn't want my quiet to offend anyone, nor did I want to offer insight into what life was like when your child is a victim of a mass shooting. That was how I felt that night at the light in front of the Stop and Shop.

I sat at the light, waiting for it to turn green, and it dawned on me: it was late, I was tired, and here I was, still going. "*Really,* God?" I mumbled. My thoughts tumbled out as they had on the pages of my journal. Only this time, I just kept going. "I am so tired of feeling this way, God. Why am I having to go to the grocery store in the middle of the night? I just want to crawl into bed and go to sleep."

It was the first time I had actually spoken real and true feelings out loud to God. Sure, I recited prayers and participated in Mass, but actually speaking spontaneous prayers to the Lord God—that was uncomfortable and intimidating. Writing my thoughts was much easier than speaking them. But there was just something about this night; at the light by the Stop and Shop— this was different. I was alone, and I was actually speaking to God. Well, it wasn't really speaking; it was more like chastising. The more I spoke, the bolder my words became.

"God, why am I the one who needs to walk on eggshells? Why am I the one left shopping in the dead of night, trying so hard to make everyone else feel better?"

The light turned green, and I did not move. I sat there, pelting God with questions. "God, do you see how tired I am? Are you ever going to send me someone who will pull me in close and say, 'No, it's not all right, and you can stop saying that now'? When is it my turn to be loved, God?"

Questions turned into comments and emotions compounded, and my voice went from mumbling to full-on accusation, bolder and braver even as the light cycled through another time.

"God, I want my family back. I want my life back. I want this whole awful nightmare to be over and to wake up to what I had. I am tired of watching Freddy wrestle. I am tired of watching an eight-year-old grieve. I am tired of seeing him pretend to be OK. I am tired of keeping this family duct-taped together, of being the strong one. You have left me here to accomplish the unthinkable—alone. And God, I feel alone, and you are supposed to know that. I want my baby back. I want to be getting ready for her seventh birthday. It was supposed to be different. She was beautiful and wanted, strong and unstoppable."

I let out a bloodcurdling scream, slammed my fists into the steering wheel, and wept as I did when Catherine first died. Then, enraged, I came in for the final blow.

Screeching, I lashed out, "I. Am. So. Angry. Supposedly you know all this, and you do . . . nothing. Here I am, trying to keep it all together. I pray. Every single day I sit at that table and pray. I keep my chin up, and I get out of bed every single day. And instead of making my life a little easier, you make it harder. Evidence? Boxes! And not just one but *two*. Two freaking evidence boxes labeled with her name. Boxes I am having to deal with because she is dead—a death you could have stopped, but didn't. Is this some cruel joke?"

And when I had said it, I just sat there, gasping for air and wiping the snot running from my nose. Within minutes, the Lord God I had only recently grown comfortable writing my thoughts and my days to had become the target of my spoken frustration, hurt, and raw pain.

When I realized what I had just done, I gasped. I had been striving not to disappoint him, and here I was at the stoplight across from Stop and Shop thinking, in the heat of a one-sided battle, that I might just have undone the effects of hundreds of hours logged at the kitchen table.

It was like an awful fight when feelings that have been stuffed into the depths of your heart escape. The moment they tumble out, the battleground goes silent in the realization that what has been said can't be taken back and whomever you are battling with might just leave.

And if it were anyone else, that might actually happen. But this is God. He knew I was wrestling. He knew the storms that I had been ignoring, and he is greater than all the storms combined.

Let's not forget: we have a God who calms the storms.

NAME YOUR STORM

Did you know, according to the National Ocean Service, that the reason we name storms is to "avoid confusion and miscommunication"? Maybe that is why we need to name our personal storms: so that *we*, not God, are clear about the tender and raw places that need his healing. Maybe it's only by facing the breakers of our hearts head-on, by naming our storms, that we can get to a place where peace can be found.

So on that night, after I had finished naming my storms, I melted into a puddle, rested my head on the steering wheel, and whispered, "Oh my God, I am sorry. Please do not hold my words against me. I beg you, forgive me. Don't leave me, because if not you, then what, then who?" I have never spoken with such depth of conviction, nor have I ever fought so hard for forgiveness.

And then, as it so often happens when two lovers battle, there is the moment when all the words needing to be spoken are said, gentle apology is offered, quiet ensues, and peace seems to hover—an unspoken understanding that everything will be all right. So it happened that night at the light at Stop and Shop. Every lie about whom I thought the Lord God could be was released from the depths of my heart, and space was made ready for the truth of who he really is.

There would be no immediate answers to the storms I named that night. The heartbreak, disappointment, and sadness I had been trying to ignore would not immediately dissipate. No, those storms would be calmed in their own time. And what I thought would be God's voice of utter disappointment or confirmation that I had colossally failed never came. No, God does not succumb to our insecurities. There would only be peace that hovered then as it does now.

So on that night, when I had cried every tear I could cry, I waited for the light to cycle to green. I never made it to the Stop and Shop. Instead, I turned around and went home. And when I arrived, I moved the boxes, the evidence boxes calling out her name, from the dining room to under the bed in her bedroom where they would stay until I was ready.

find your sanctuary

> · Consider it all joy, my brothers, when you
> encounter various trials, for you know that
> the testing of your faith produces perse-
> verance. And let perseverance be perfect,
> so that you may be perfect and complete,
> lacking in nothing.
>
> —James 1:2–4

1. Evidence boxes were the things that tested my faith
    and brought me to a place of readiness. Have you
    ever had a definitive turning point like this in your faith
    journey? How did your reaction change the course of
    that journey?
2. What is your initial reaction to my experience at the
    stoplight at the Stop and Shop? Have you ever spoken
    to God with your true, uncensored self?
3. "Maybe that is why we need to name our storms: so
    that *we*, not God, are clear about the tender and raw
    places that need his healing." What storms do you
    need to name?

CHAPTER 5

the arduous journey

I started running again after Catherine died. I hadn't run since college, so I'm not at all sure why I suddenly had the urge to lace up my running shoes again. But I did, and there I was taking to the streets and to the treadmill in the bowels of my basement, just wanting to run far and run fast.

When I first set out, three miles felt like a marathon that left me rattled, huffing, puffing, and convinced my lungs would explode. Slowly over time, three miles turned into six, eight, and eventually thirteen.

Now, it may sound like an effortless process and that I am now some incredible runner who laces up and races down the street as the sun rises over the horizon. I'm sure that happens— just not with me. For the first three miles, I'm a hot mess. Those miles are brutal; I'm clunky and spend the whole time wondering what on earth possessed me to utter the words *love* and *run* in the same sentence.

And yet I have also come to understand that, no matter how awkward they may be, those first three miles serve a purpose: they prepare me for what is ahead. Now that I know that, I do not fight them.

So there I was one morning, pounding away on the treadmill and listening to Fr. Mike Schmitz on the *Ascension Presents* podcast. He was talking about what it means to be steadfast.

The words jolted me. They made such complete sense and brought what I had been struggling with into immediate and sharp focus. With an inelegant move, I straddled the treadmill's moving belt and planted my feet onto the side rails, not wanting to miss a vowel of what was being spoken.

Then I hit the back arrow and listened to it all again. It was a discussion about faith being built with intention and purpose—faith is built with steadfast resolve to claim the victory. Fr. Schmitz said faith is grown in a way that is not unlike the way premier athletes train. Their muscles are intentionally stretched and sometimes torn. Athletes take to the gym, the field, or the road and purposefully push themselves further than the last time they were in that very spot. And when they are done, they rest—but only for so long before returning to the very same place and doing it all over again until it becomes second nature.

Any other point in my life, I would have heard it as exactly what an athlete in training does and moved on. But this morning I got the message loud and clear: the athlete is me, the muscle is my heart, and what I was going through was somehow making me steadfast.

Down in my basement, I received an answer to one of the many questions I had launched at my heavenly Father at Stop and Shop's stoplight. The constant reminders that Catherine was gone, the milestones and memories, and the storm clouds that were collecting and pressing me to the limit were absolutely necessary.

The break I begged God to give me would have defeated the victory. The very thing that had challenged and chafed and stretched me, God wanted to use for my faith, just as training pushes an athlete's body to the brink.

My heavenly Father knows my limits and knew I was strong enough to face what I was facing at that moment. I was only being made stronger so as to become steadfast and lack nothing. I just needed to reach a point that I could believe in myself the way my Lord God believed in me.

A SEASON OF FIRSTS

I was in the season of firsts. But this was nothing like a birthday, prom, graduation, or marriage. Nope. I had no idea what to do with these firsts. I'd never dealt with them before, and frankly, those who had been here hadn't really shared their experience in too much detail.

I think I know why. The first time you experience something with or without whatever *it* may be—for me, it was celebrating without Catherine—draws a line in the sand that assures you *it* really did happen. Time has marched forward, and there is no room to negotiate any of it. Firsts are brutally hard and left me with a pit in my stomach thinking the exact same day and experience would return 365 days from now. These firsts were, for me, like my first runs after Catherine died: clunky, awkward, and leaving me bent over sucking air.

Mother's Day and Easter were precursors to what was coming: June 8. Catherine's birthday. It would be the first birthday since she died, and with it came a whole new level of emotion I really hadn't anticipated or yet experienced.

For me, other people's birthdays are a big deal. They mark the day that God intentionally placed a soul onto the earth with a purpose so real and potential so great that they contribute to his greater good and plan for his kingdom. Every single one of us—you and me, the baby placed in our care, a friend in our midst, or the lover in our arms—is intentionally placed on this earth with a divine purpose.

So given that birthdays are the day divine has the potential to shine even brighter on earth, my hope has always been that Catherine knew and Freddy knows the day they graced this earth is a day like none other. It is a big deal.

Every year, Catherine's birthday started on Mother's Day, when she began to wrestle with what would be that year's party theme. Every year she would try to convince me that an "all the animals" party would be completely doable. It would take a full week of assuring her I couldn't do right by her "all the animals" party. Eventually, we would land on a more manageable idea and be off to the races.

From the design of the invitation that would promise a very special celebration to the party favor her favorite people would carry home, every detail soon took space in my house and my heart. I would spend weeks working late into the night, long after she had fallen asleep, creating all that she had imagined when she described what she saw her party looking like. On her birthday, I wanted her to look around and know dreams can, in fact, be realized.

In what felt like both a blink and a year, the day of Catherine's birthday celebration would arrive, and every crevice of the house oozed with what she had imagined and described. The dining room's threshold would welcome all her favorite people to a table overflowing with all that had been collected, curated, and crafted. The balloons would fill every inch of the room's ceiling. And when all her favorite people had settled in, it felt as if the entire house had erupted in a belly laugh, confirming this was indeed a day worthy of celebration—that her being born was a really big deal.

And then, just like that, the last favor was handed off and it was over. The house returned to its pre–Mother's Day rhythm, and I would be left exhausted.

And so I braced myself for the unknown in the weeks leading up to June 8, 2013. There would be no collecting, curating, or crafting for a backyard celebration. Instead, I found myself replaying every single birthday we had ever celebrated while she graced the earth—starting with the day she was born. The rush of memories caught me off guard then, but it is a rush that I have come to embrace.

The morning she was born, she arrived quickly and with an undeniable determination. As she slept beside me, she radiated a peace and warmth I had never experienced. To this day as her birthday approaches, I can feel her warmth.

Now when Catherine's birthday approaches, the milestone emblazoned in red Sharpie on the calendar, I have learned that for those weeks leading up to the day, I will exist in two parallel times: the present and the past as memories of previous birthdays replay as if they are being lived in the moment. The memories rush and flood and at times overwhelm. Sometimes I have to catch my breath in the realization of how much I miss my baby girl and how much my life has dramatically changed without her.

So what do you do—what did I do—when the flood of memories threatens to overwhelm? I can assure you, what I did with them on Catherine's seventh birthday was, for me, not the right answer.

When the day I had been dreading arrived, I agreed that we would celebrate it quietly by doing something Catherine would have loved to do. So on that morning, we packed the car, made a pit stop at the cemetery, and went to the zoo. We meandered on the trails and stopped at the exhibits we had seen with Catherine. I was sluggish, and it was quiet and sad. There was no backyard celebration, and there were no favorite people gathered togeth-er—in my opinion, this was hardly a celebration for the soul who graced the earth that very day. As we drove home from the zoo, I searched the heavens as if I would find her perched on a cloud and vowed that day would never feel disappointing again. Her birthday would be celebrated because, on this day that she graced the earth, the stars shone a little brighter.

Days circled in red Sharpie on the calendar are remarkable days—be they birthdays, holidays, or special family days that become like holidays. If they were not remarkable, why would they be circled? Wrapped in these remarkable days are the tradi-tions and celebrations that scream this is the day: "This is the day the Lord has made; let us rejoice in it and be glad" (Ps 118:24). When honored, these are the very days that strengthen a tender heart to claim the victory of joy.

I know this because of the bus cake. Of all things—*a bus cake.*

THE BUS CAKE

Every year for the first day of school I make a futile attempt to transform two cakes into some semblance of a school bus. Every year I start out with ambition and intention, thinking this is the year that it all will click, and the result will be a bus worthy of the cover of a food magazine. Yellow frosting, white windows—it goes great until the last bit of black frosting needs to be piped to frame the windows and create the doors and wheels.

When I break out the tube of black frosting, it's over.

It is pitiful. At this point the bus cake goes from road worthy to junkyard.

The bus cake has never had what you would consider wheels. Wheels!? They are circles that I just can't get right. It's going on twelve years of creating these less-than-masterful masterpieces, and I have come to accept it will never pass as suitable for transport even to and from some imaginary school in the land of sweet.

Sadly, before Catherine died, that simple fact would have kept me up at night—kind of like the Christmas picture had. I was fixated on making everything I did perfect.

Not so much anymore. I have come to realize it is not about the bus cake but about what the bus cake stands for. The bus cake made its first appearance when Freddy started preschool. It marked a celebration of what would be the first of many firsts, a tangible symbol of the eager anticipation of all the opportunities a new school year will bring.

Freddy was then starting fourth grade. It was a new beginning, a fresh start at a new school. He would be considered part of the upper grade, and that was something to celebrate. But now the question loomed in my mind: would there be a bus cake when he came home, as there had always been?

I was wrestling a new wrestling match that replaced the pre-dawn getting-out-of-bed match. No one would have been the wiser if I hadn't made it, and I am sure if it weren't sitting on the counter when my son came home, he would have never uttered a word.

It's that way with every first after the *it* that changed your world: deciding whether to put up the Christmas tree; whether to attempt a birthday celebration on the day they were born, even though they are now dead; or how you will mark the anniversary of the day everything changed. The reality is, the days are circled in red because they stand for something important, and for that reason alone, they need to be acknowledged—even if at first it's a bit awkward.

And so, because of what I realized with the *first* birthday-after-she-died fiasco, I knew I had to make the bus cake. My heart knew, as hard as this might be, traditions that filled years of love must be honored, even when it seemed impossible. That meant making the bus cake—even though Catherine would not be there to cut into it with Freddy.

So I did it. I sent Freddy off to school, and I stood in the kitchen going through the motions of creating my not-so-masterful masterpiece as the previous six years of first days of school played through my head.

I stopped on the one just one year before.

It was her first day of a full school day—she was officially a first grader. She was excited about what the year would bring and afraid of being away from me for a full day.

As I spread the yellow icing across what was supposedly the roof of the bus, I thought about our annual pilgrimage to check off the list of school supplies they would need for the school year. It was our thing—a daylong event: school supply shopping, lunch out, and figuring out what was still left to do on our summer bucket list to be able to call it the "best summer ever."

Shopping for school supplies was a process and tested my patience. Freddy just wanted it done, while Catherine made each selection with intention and purpose. She'd search the shelves looking for the notebooks and folders whose covers displayed the cutest puppy, kitten, or most beautiful dog she could find. I'd stand back and let her do her thing, knowing these creatures would be her friends smiling back at her at those times when she had tear-stained cheeks during the next 183 days. For her, school supplies were more than a tool for learning. They were an accessory—an extension of her soul. For me, these notebooks, folders, and trinkets offered a small bit of hope they might make her smile during days I knew she struggled. I can still picture the folder she was so excited finding: it had a chocolate Lab wearing beads and a boa. She gasped at how cute this was and had to have it.

As I frosted the cake, I gasped in the realization the very folder that caused her to gasp was among the things tucked carefully into the boxes I had moved from the dining room to under her bed. The mere thought shook me to the core.

I could not get the thought out of my head. Her things were in the boxes under her bed, and I needed to see them. It was as if those boxes had magnets drawing me in. I abandoned my futile attempts to create a bus and climbed the steps that led to her room.

FACING THE BOXES

Her room was—and still is—as it was the day she died. Until the bus cake day, there were mornings that I would sit at her desk and pore over the treasures she tucked into the drawers and little cubby, but I would never linger long.

On that morning, though, I sat on her floor as I had done when she was alive. It was where we would talk and play and dream. I sat on the floor beside her bed and carefully pulled box 1 of 2 from under it. I held my breath lifting its cover.

At the top of the box was her backpack with purple "CVH" embroidered initials. I lifted the backpack from the box and unzipped its front panel, finding her friends—the stuffed animals I told her she could take to school only if they could fit in this very space and stay there. And there they were, just as she assured me. They were tucked in along with her trinkets; the things that at one time made me shake my head now all of a sudden were the sacred artifacts I piled in my lap as the tears I'd been holding onto streamed down my face.

Her coat was next. It had been folded just below the backpack. Less than a year ago, it seemed too big, and now it looked too small. Tucked into the coat's pockets were her little mittens—just as I had taught her to do. She had been afraid she would lose them. "What then?" she asked me plaintively.

"Keep them in your pockets," I told her. "When your hands get cold and you put them in your pockets, your mittens will be waiting to hold them." I pulled the coat into my arms as if she were in it. I put the mittens in my hands as if hers were in them. The backpack, her treasures, her coat, and her mittens—it was all just too much. I curled into a ball on the floor and let all that I had been holding onto go, weeping with an intensity I had not had in a very long time.

I am not sure at what point it happened, but I fell asleep. Right there on her floor where she and I had sat for hours, talking and playing, I finally slept deeply and soundly for hours. When I woke up, her coat was pulled tightly to my chest and her backpack was tucked into my lap. Every muscle in my body felt as if it had been clenched for years. Even with eyes swollen and a heart broken, there was stillness in that room that settled my soul, and for the very first time, I felt at peace.

I pushed myself up off the floor, tucked the treasures back into the backpack, and folded the coat. I loaded the box in the same way I emptied it: backpack first and then, with palm flat as if I was pushing a kiss into her heart, her coat. I returned the lid of box 1 of 2, slid it under the bed, and made my way downstairs.

Freddy would soon be home.

By the time he walked in the door, the bus cake was finished and sitting on the counter. He stopped in his tracks. I wasn't sure if he didn't expect it to be there, had forgotten the bus cake was something that we did, or thought it was something we did only with Catherine. Whatever it was, he looked me in the eye and said, "Thank you, Mama."

And with that, life fell into its school routine and I was bracing for the triple-crown threat still ahead: Halloween, Thanksgiving, and Christmas. And that didn't even include the anniversary thrown right in the middle of it all. The memories would be biting and deliver the hard-hitting punches in knowing there was a time when at that very moment in the past Catherine was here, physically here, with me on this earth.

I had learned with the bus cake that as hard as it was to do, the traditions built around the dates marked with Sharpie on a calendar are important and must be honored. They hurt and test an already-broken heart. They will suck oxygen from lungs, and yet in some strange way, the same way an athlete willingly shows up to be broken down, they will strengthen. It seems counter-intuitive, but so is the idea that a muscle torn will heal stronger.

Let's not forget that the heart is a muscle.

That year of firsts, the Halloween decorations were put out and the bats that always hung from the dining room chandelier were hung, although we forgot to carve the pumpkins on our front steps. Thanksgiving dinner was made, albeit in a faraway place, and with very few people, we bowed our heads and gave thanks. And the Christmas tree was set up—although in a different room. We adorned it with as many decorations as we could muster, and when Freddy said, "I think that's good," it was good. It may not have been the full court press that it was in years past, but it was a start.

I have often wondered, if I had not made the bus cake that day, would I have ever made it again? The answer I always come back to is no. And frankly, if I had somehow rationalized not making the bus cake, it would have been easier to walk away from the triple-crown threat that followed. And that would have been a travesty.

I think this is what athletes know. I think they know in their gut, if they shy away from the training that burns their muscles and breaks their body, their ability to claim the victory for what-ever it is they are training for is no longer so certain.

They intuitively know they are only made stronger in their breaking.

And it is the same for us on this long, arduous journey, with whatever the *it* we may be walking with. These milestones marked are the blunt reminder there was a time they were with you or *it* was not even a thought to be considered. It was the very thing that brought me to collapsing in the middle of my baby girl's room, crying the ugly cry that left my body wrecked and eyes swollen.

As upside down as this may seem, these are the very things that strengthen us and are not meant to be shied away from.

It seems so surprising, but we are assured of this. "Do not fear: I am with you; do not be anxious: I am your God. I will strengthen you, I will help you, I will uphold you with my victorious right hand" (Is 41:10).

In the months that followed, I would be strengthened sitting on her floor, boxes open, each time more and more of their contents spread across the floor. Over the years, the Christmas tree seems to hold more and more ornaments and Halloween seems to get a little spookier and Thanksgiving more thankful. In honoring the milestones of my journey with Catherine walking with me, my heart is made stronger in the journey I must continue to walk now that she is gone.

In this knowing, I resolve to acknowledge the milestones and memories and trust that in the pain they most certainly always bring, I will be strengthened and transformed. You see, my beautiful friend, I believe this is what it means to be steadfast: to stand firm in that which breaks our hearts, knowing it will ultimately transform them. And I now know that we must be trained in being steadfast. We are all very much like the athletes that face the trial: they are well equipped to claim the victory for it is the moment they trained for.

Steadfast is how we claim the victory in our trials, how we discover a deep-rooted joy and realize we lack nothing.

I know now I needed to be trained to run this race with steadfast endurance, and this run is not finished. And some days that is a hard thing to wrap my head around, because I know that will include more suffering. What I know, though, and what I often need to remind myself is that when I do suffer and remain steadfast in trusting it is the very thing that is strengthening me, I will lack nothing.

On the day I made the bus cake and Freddy came home and stopped short seeing it on the counter, when he looked at me and said, "Thank you, Mama," there was a spark in his eyes. A spark I had not seen in a very long time. When I saw it, I knew—I claimed a victory, one of many victories.

find your sanctuary

Do not fear: I am with you;
    do not be anxious: I am your God.
I will strengthen you, I will help you,
    I will uphold you with my victorious right
    hand.
—Isaiah 41:10

1. What do you do that you force yourself to do? How has it built steadfastness?
2. "I have often wondered, if I had not made the bus cake that day, would I have ever made it again? The answer I always come back to is no." To what have you said the hard yes and knew it was a turning point?

3. Consider your victories. What is the intangible, non-manufactured reward?

CHAPTER 6

companions
along the way

There was a route I walked with a friend that became so familiar I can still walk it with my eyes closed. As we walked in the early days after Catherine died, I would tell her about the stares I'd learned to accept and my goal of acknowledging each and every remembrance of Catherine that we had received.

On one of those walks she said innocently, "You will get really good at asking for and accepting help." When she said that to me, my stomach lurched. I didn't like being told with such certainty that I would be compelled to learn how to do the very thing that made me most uncomfortable. Not after going through all this.

Her comment reminded me of the very essence of Halloween. Yes, Halloween! What does Halloween have to do with being comfortable asking for and accepting help? For me, Halloween had never been about reinventing myself in a costume and marching confidently door to door, eagerly presenting a plastic pumpkin to an unknown homeowner ready to offer me a bite-size nugget of candy. I had certainly never experienced the eager and expected joy of dumping a filled-to-the-brim plastic pumpkin on the living room floor.

Oh no, Halloween made me feel like a charity case; I dreaded standing there with my hands out, eagerly receiving a handout. Handouts, as I had been taught, were neither acceptable nor allowed. My life experiences had taught me that before I could request and receive help, I had to meet two clear prerequisites: (1) I had to have worked my hardest to get what I needed for myself, and (2) I would be honor-bound to repay what I had received—in full. And if I could do both, my request proved worthy of occupying someone else's time and attention.

That became a bit tricky where God was concerned. The way I saw it, I could never say with complete confidence, "I worked hard enough." In my mind, there was always something else I could have done, more hours I could have invested in both the doing that led to my asking and the repaying that would be required because of it. And anyway, how on earth could I ever repay the God of the universe?

It was rare that anything I did was enough, and therefore, anything I received was, by default, a handout that evoked feelings not of exuberant joy but of shame. What was worse, I had no clue that I had become trapped in a catastrophic cycle that was chipping away at the very fiber of my being and the worth I should have held in confidence in the crevices of my heart.

Perhaps that is why my friend's comment caused my tangled mess of emotions to tighten my stomach into a knot. The slightest hint of anything that involved receiving help, advice, gifts, and compliments was painful and excruciatingly hard to accept. My own birthday was especially hard to bear because it involved receiving gifts I was sure I didn't deserve. Even a simple compliment was brushed aside; a simple *thank you* just didn't seem enough, for words themselves felt false. I convinced myself they were something people would just say because they felt they had to—because I couldn't attribute them to myself. Over time, every single denial and sweep of an arm put my own worth out of my own reach and understanding.

Worth. It comes down to an understanding of worth, of living in the truth and understanding of who I am as a daughter of God, the source of every good gift.

I understand that truth now. Over time and in the space that has been since Catherine's death, I can hold my own gaze in the mirror and see a woman *beloved* and *worthy.* I can see that now, but I did not fully understand this when Catherine died. And the reality is, I am still a work in process—that process by which the things I believe in my head nestle their way into my heart. I have come to believe it takes a lifetime to truly understand these things. I think if we really understood whose we are and see ourselves with eyes as he sees us, we would act differently. Very, very differently.

And I do, act differently. Well, now I do.

Before Catherine died, I knew with my mind that I belonged to God, but my heart was telling a very different story. Worth is a heart matter, and that would take some figuring out.

BACK TO THE GARDEN

I know that the One who scatters the stars, paints the skies, and halts the waters at sandy shores created me with the purpose of tending to his garden. The fact that I was created by the Almighty and that his creation was labeled by the Creator as good I will never fully comprehend. But this is the case for me, and it is for you too.

But don't take my word for it—read Genesis.

> Then the LORD God formed the man out of the dust
> of the ground and blew into his nostrils the breath of

> life, and the man became a living being. . . . The LORD
> God then took the man and settled him in the garden
> of Eden, to cultivate and care for it. (Gn 2:7, 15)

We were created to be stewards of all of creation. That, in itself, is an awesome and humbling responsibility.

For six years my garden was graced with a little girl who taught me more than I could have ever taught her, and that garden continues to bear fruit in the life of a beautiful boy whom I watch grow in stature and wisdom and being afforded opportunities that I would have never imagined. My cup has been filled so much; I should press my hand over its rim and proclaim, "I need no more."

I don't need more, but that is not where this story ends. My garden has continued to expand, as God has fulfilled my deepest desires—desires that he has encouraged me to express to him boldly and with eager anticipation, knowing they will be given.

There was a time I would have been unable to do this, afraid that I was unworthy to ask. However, because of what I have been through, I am no longer afraid to ask. But before I could ask boldly, I needed to tend to the matters of my heart, to see myself through the eyes of my Father, and to know my own worth. This, too, is something Catherine taught me—not in life but through her death. She taught me to see God in a new way—for who he is and not just who I thought he was.

I share this next statement in all humility: I had it all wrong. I had seen God as a begrudging giver of "handouts" to those who never put a foot out of line. I was convinced he judged me for what I had and had not done and ruled from afar with the expectation that I needed to strive harder before he would even consider granting what my heart hungered for.

That God doesn't exist—thankfully.

THE "FINE" LIFE

Being a mother has helped me realize how far off my understanding really was. And isn't that the way it goes sometimes? We have to walk in another's shoes to get it? At least for me it was that way—I discovered his heart in the heart I have for my children.

At times, Freddy assures me he is fine. Depending on the way he says "It's fine" and "I'm fine," I know how much truth he speaks. Sometimes his "I'm fine" echoes my voice—flat and noncommittal. I get that *fine* because I often live there too: there is food on the table, clothes on our backs, and a roof overhead. But there is more to life than that, so much more, and he knows it as much as I know it. If we didn't, our voices wouldn't be so flat when we said the word *fine* like an arrow of disappointment that flies across the bow.

Fine, I have come to realize, is code for *safe*. Fine is what happens when we settle for well enough, not sure that asking for more is appropriate or will even be answered. It's a question of whether our hearts could possibly stand one more disappointment, and sometimes it's best to not be disappointed and just be safe.

But there are times that I can see further and more clearly than what Freddy sees. I know he will not be disappointed, that he has nothing to fear and everything to celebrate, and that agreeing to "it's fine" offers nothing but a detour around a blessing so close that not receiving it would be a colossal fail.

It was like that on the day we were on the highway and he told me he was going to throw up and couldn't go to football tryouts. He had me so convinced that I had changed lanes and set my sights on the next exit that would allow us to turn back home. I was ready to acquiesce until I heard him say it in a way that I just knew.

"I'm fine, let's just turn around. I don't need to play football." The way he said it pressed the red alert button. It was not fine, and I assured him that this was something that he *could do*. I uttered every descriptor that I knew of him and his heart, desperately wanting him to live in the truth of what I saw in him and who he was.

When we were close to arriving, I shot the final arrow back across the deck. I looked over at him and said, "Freddy, you've been talking about trying out for the football team for a long time now. If it's something you really want, you need to walk in the confidence of whose you are. If this is something you want to do—and I believe you do—go get it; it's yours for the taking. You have the full power of your God with you and for you. And that makes you worthy enough to walk on that field."

And with that and whatever confidence he could muster, he walked tentatively down the path and tried out for a team and sport that he had never played—never. Not once.

And he made it. Not only did he make the team but also he played varsity and lettered. My heart breaks to think he was so close to not realizing the confidence and assurance that he gained from the season of taking to that field. All of it—every last bit—could have been lost by taking the exit I was headed toward. But it's more than confidence or a letter that he now wears proudly on a jacket. It's not even making the team for a sport that he had never even played before that day that brings me to tears every time I contemplate it.

It is in the knowing.

I love that sunk into his heart is an understanding. He may not see it that way now, but someday he will. He experienced at fifteen what I had just started learning at forty-five. He is worthy, not because of the letter he earned but because he is the son of the Almighty.

He is worthy. He is the son of the Creator of the entire universe. I've known that as truth for my son since the day he was born. I spoke it over him at every opportunity.

I needed to know this for myself as well, and it would take people holding the hand I was using to cover the rim of my cup assuring me I was fine, that my life was as full as it could be, to understand there is so much more room left for it to be filled to overflowing.

COMPANIONS OF GRIEF

One of the aspects of grief that continued to weigh on me in the years following Catherine's death was the weight of other people's grief. At times their comments cut deep, and at other times, I felt as if I were drowning when, in reality, a way was being made for the companions who were gathering.

"You've changed" came the subtle accusation from family and friends in the months and years after Catherine died. I was told I wasn't accessible; they didn't feel a priority. I had turned my back; I was not doing what I should.

They were right. I *had* changed. How could I have not? You cannot bury your baby and not be a different person from that experience. Yet their words were darts that wreaked havoc on my already raw and broken heart. Periods of accusations would turn into periods of silence—stone-cold silence—and that just about killed me. At a time when the silence in my house was already deafening and we were all trying to make sense of the hurt we were feeling, I was offered more silence. Suffering took on a new meaning. My marriage was suffering, family relationships were suffering, and I was suffocating.

During this time of silence, I encountered the first of many companions who would travel this long and, at times, lonely journey, companions who did things out of love and not out of a sense of obligation. Their gentle companionship is what made it possible for the changes to come full circle, into a healing place.

Freddy and I pulled onto our road, an already long afternoon—it was a Thursday, and on Thursday we went to counseling. I sighed deeply, not knowing whose car was now parked in front of the house. I braced myself and reached for my phone, thinking it was one of those intrusive curiosity seekers, strangers who clearly believed they had the right to see what our lives had become in the aftermath of the school shooting. They would sit in the cul-de-sac, waiting for us to walk out the front door or drive by, their camera poised to snap a photo. It was bizarre and something I still can't understand.

So when I spotted that unknown car, my first impulse was to call the state trooper who had taken us under his watch. But then the person in the car saw us coming and got out. This was no gawking stranger; it was my brother, the very one who had driven through the night to get to me when Catherine died. Now he had flown in when I had gone quiet, just shown up without expectation or fanfare.

Please do not misunderstand. I am not insinuating that my family didn't come to visit, because they did. It was what we all did: we kept our unspoken promises to one another and were there for each other at every wedding and every funeral—including my baby girl's. Trips were planned and communicated in advance; arrivals were always announced. We always knew what to expect.

But now, there he was, sitting in the cul-de-sac. It was so unexpected, a spontaneous expression of concern and solidarity. It wasn't promised or planned, and it certainly was not announced. He stood in the road and said he was worried and simply needed to see me and Freddy. I ushered him into the house, and he choked back tears; he could barely speak the words he had written to me so often: "I am so sorry; you need to know that I am with you, and I am for you."

His choked words were God's whispered truth. A truth I would hear over and over again from those God placed in my path—not just family but true companions.

Even as I write this, I am astounded at the mercy of it all. I'm not sure what prompted him to come. Maybe God knew my heart and that I would easily question his whisper, rationalizing my worth as less than it is. Maybe I would simply shrug it off as "well, that is just what family does." They show up when they are expected. They circle the wagons and hoist the flags.

True companionship, real friendship, is something altogether different. There are different kinds of friends; I experienced that in such a powerful way when Catherine died. There were friendships I held close well before Catherine even graced this earth, those that were formed when I was a young mother, and those that were forged because she died; each of these companions speak truth in their own special and beautiful way. I just didn't see it in the moment.

Before Catherine died, it made me wholly uncomfortable if a friend circled the wagons and hoisted the flags for me—though of course I would do it for them in an instant. I would do anything for my friends; I would run away and stand witness at a wedding on a cold February day or would work late into the night to make sure I would not let my peers down. But knowing the same would be done in return for me left me with the familiar knot in my stomach as I listened to the lies of my old, familiar friend "handout."

I needed truth spoken to me and over me by companions coming alongside me to discover it, much like the truth that was discovered on the road to Emmaus. I needed companions who would bear the face of Jesus, tending to my broken heart, acknowledging my disappointments, and urging me to press forward. These very people speak truth powerfully and from a place of love, especially when my urge to take the very next exit, turn around, and head back home is greatest. These are the people who look me in the eye and assure me that would be a huge mistake.

And having companions along the way would not be an all-or-nothing notion as I was often inclined to believe. Some companions would journey for a very short time; others, for a season; and still others, for a lifetime.

SCATTERED AND SEASONAL COMPANIONS

There were those companions who walked with me for a very short time; I was certain they scattered because it was just too hard to be around me, whether due to my grief or theirs. With scattering companions, I realized my worth like a house of glass that would inevitably form cracks and shatter, wrapped up as it was in their acceptance.

Eventually, it did shatter of course. And I am better for it. The shattering walls opened a way for my heart, the one I felt unworthy of sharing, to be seen for what it was.

An exposed heart is a vulnerable heart. And when a vulnerable heart feels a shard of shattered glass, it hurts. It hurts a lot.

But trust me, once the shards of those walls are removed and that vulnerable heart is unconfined, you will be offered a love whose depth and breadth are immeasurable and unceasing.

Not all companions ran away of course. Some joined me deliberately for just a season, walking with me until we reached a shared destination—knowing at that point we would part ways. And that is also something that breaks my heart. Goodbyes do not come easy for me. And yet, these are the companions who taught me of a love that is unwavering and a knowing that will continually unfold.

And then there are the companions I know I will have for a lifetime. The day I went to the nursery to gather the plants to adorn Catherine's gravesite was the beginning of one such friendship, a beautiful friendship that emerged and would teach me more about myself than I dared to believe was possible and speak truth I had not heard in a very long time. Her friendship would fill me with confidence that would give me eyes to see and a heart to repel what is not authentic and to pull closer what is.

The trip to the nursery slowly became lunches that would linger long into the afternoon until Freddy was due home from school. We would laugh over life stories and map out adventures we were convinced we should take and chart out obstacles we would conquer. She brought me to the place she called her "safe haven" in hopes that I would find the peace and serenity she knew it could offer to a soul that desperately needed it. Through her, I was blessed to find a kind of sacred sanctuary.

Slowly, over time, our friendship grew and was brought to a place where I understood what it looks like and know what it feels like when a raw and vulnerable heart is shared in confidence and received in love. And once I did, there was no accepting anything less.

She asked me in all seriousness, "What do you want? What do you want more than anything?" I breathed deeply, knowing

this was a moment that had the potential to define this friendship as authentic, appointed, and divine. This was a crossroads
moment such as I described earlier, where love embraces the
broken, protects the most fragile parts, and dances in delight
of every single victory. It is where you choose to be true and
authentic or safe and guarded.

I could have said in response to her question, *To see my
Freddy realize his dream*. Or, *for a marriage that is slipping away
to grow in love and grace*. Or I could have said I wanted to see
the relationships that had been strained, restored; or the project
I was working on, succeed. And if I said any of those things, they
would be truth—I wanted them all. They were on my list in the
back of my journal. But they were not what I wanted more than
anything, and we were speaking the truth of my heart.

My eyes welled and spilled over. I looked straight into her
eyes and said, "I want to be loved."

There it was, out in open view—my heart exposed with what
it most desired. I did not feel loved. I had not for a long time.
The only place where I encountered an overwhelming sense of
being loved and valued was when I was with my two children,
one of whom had been killed. I felt forsaken and had told God
as much, and now I was sharing this little-known fact with a
newfound friend.

I waited for the condemnation, but what I heard and saw was
the face and the voice of God. She looked at me, her eyes spilling
over, and whispered, "I know."

And I believe she knew. She had spent months then, and
years now, listening to my heart.

I believe God knew that moment would come, and her weeping was his heart breaking that I did not know his love. I believe
God knows our hearts better than we can even imagine. He
knew mine was breaking before I could even put words to the
emotions that I wrestled and was forming his response well in

advance so that when I could put words to what I was feeling, I would be met with his gentle voice and overflowing eyes.

In truths spoken and trust offered in the years since that afternoon, our friendship has been filled to overflowing time and again, and the lessons I learned would spill into other friendships, training me to accept love and the truth in the path I was created to walk.

A FRIEND JUST FOR ME

I met another treasured companion on a school trip with my son. She did not blink when I shared Catherine had been one of the victims of the Sandy Hook shooting. It was a part of my story I had grown accustomed to stopping just shy of sharing. Sometimes it was just easier to say, "I have two children," and quickly change the subject to avoid giving more detail. And yet with her it was easy to share the not-so-easy details of my life.

This friend taught me to do things just for me. She found out that, like her, I was a runner, so we ran together, not on the hills of the town we lived but rather on the sandy shores of the place she loved. She convinced me that it would be a trip of a lifetime. She had the perfect place, and I was excited for the first time in a long time. This was not a trip for work or with family or to see family. I was going just because we wanted to go.

We decided we would run a half marathon because we could, and we did. We packed up, laced up, and set off. And when we accomplished what we had set out to do, we sat, feet up on the railing, watching the day turn to night, disclosing our hurts and heartbreaks, dreams and desires. We would laugh and cry, and I would be reminded that my true and authentic heart was worthy for no other reason than it was mine—that was enough.

Our friendship grew as she traveled the world. She would return with treasures from abroad, and I was convinced she would see me as a taker on the prowl for what she was giving—a person looking for handouts.

And well, you know how that story plays out in my life.

The first time she pulled the bag from her purse saying, "Look, I found this for you on my trip," I panicked at receiving an unexpected gift. The bag was not labeled with any acknowledged date circled in red Sharpie on the calendar, and I had nothing stashed away to give in return. I was caught off guard and sure she would walk away feeling as if she drew the short straw in this friendship.

But no. That was a lie, a big fat lie whispered from my old friend "handout." She had brought me the gift because she knew my heart, and hers had been stirred to remember it.

I took the gift she offered, and she was right, I was delighted. And as hard as it was, I did not run out to get her something in return. That is the point: Love given out of love expects nothing but a hand and a heart willing to receive. The love she shares makes me want to give in return. Just as she makes me feel loved and remembered, I hope I do for all those whom I love.

COMPANIONS OF
THE HEART

I have been shown something about God through the companions I have met along the way: hands that receive with palms opened, trusting to the heavens in the One from whom the gift is coming, will never be slapped. Never. Because our Savior took that punishment on our behalf.

You are God's chosen, he assures me in words and actions. This confirmation wipes away the thought of defeat that threatens to take hold of me. I stare at the stars and realize there can be no debate. *Go get it*, he tells me, just as I told Freddy. And I do. I am strong enough to do this, and my dream is within my grasp.

With the Lord God, every attempt to hold back the swell of tears and pretense that all is fine is just plain futile. An attended-to heart cannot hide. And the truth he speaks attends to my heart.

Over time, I would learn it is best to just blurt it out—all of it: my disappointment, joy, hurt, and fear, and what warms my heart and what breaks it, confident in knowing that God, my companion, will receive it for what it is: a tender and exposed heart. He is my sanctuary.

It bothers me that it took losing Catherine to understand this. But then again, maybe matters of the heart are so important that they need to be cultivated. They are the seeds that our Lord God presses into our accepting palms, knowing we are capable stewards. We are offered the opportunity to care for, tend gently, and nurture our relationships, knowing they have the potential to flourish and fill the garden. Seeds pressed into my palm are plentiful: my brother waiting in a car in the cul-de-sac because he understands silence is not at all *fine* and lingering lunches where stories come easily and build trust to a point where questions are answered truthfully and gifts come from a place of delight and not obligation.

I have been prayed over and have prayed with these friends of mine. I have been assured that the very things I am most afraid of are figments of my imagination and that what I question as the voice of God is truly the voice of God. I have sat with them in teahouses and coffee shops, at kitchen tables and on the couch, rediscovering the sound of true laughter. And there were still others who sat beside me in the pews, silent in the stillness of prayer.

These are the companions who have provided the answer to the question with which I have wrestled and that my heart most desires. Their eyes reflect back to me the reality of whose I am and to whom I walk.

It is a deepening of a relationship with the One I will never be able to repay, One I am wholly unworthy of receiving. And he knows this and does not care because he doesn't need my repayment. He needs my heart—he desires my heart—the one he knows is true and authentic to that which it was created, so that it may tend to whatever might be the piece of his garden it has been allocated, trusting that he is ever present, where nothing need be hidden—as it was in the very beginning.

find your sanctuary

Therefore every loyal person should pray
        to you
    in time of distress.
Though flood waters threaten,
    they will never reach him.
You are my shelter; you guard me from
        distress;
    with joyful shouts of deliverance you sur-
        round me.
                                    —Psalm 32:6–7

1. There was a time I saw God as one who gave "hand-outs" only to those who had proven themselves worthy. Over time and through friendships, I have experienced the reality of God's presence and belonging to him as his beloved. How has your impression of God evolved over time?

2. Who have been your "companions"—seasonal and enduring, visible and invisible—in your greatest times

of distress? Who has walked with you through the floodwaters and kept you from drowning?

3. If you read the verses preceding this passage of Psalm 32, you will see reference to an acknowledgment of past guilt and of the sin that creates unwanted distance between us and God. The Sacrament of Reconciliation can be a place of true sanctuary for us even if we simply need a place to express our pain and doubt. Have you experienced this?

CHAPTER 7

a wild and winding path to forgiveness

I was leaning into my faith, and scripture was coming alive. The more places I sought the Lord God—even in the Old Testament—the more places I found him waiting for me. Jacob delivered my ladder, and Moses uttered my insecurities; the Israelites grumbled my gripes, and David offered praises for my joy and prayers for my pleading. They shared my fears and the same exact desires. In those holy pages I found my people, and I found my Jesus.

I read every single word of scripture intently, not taking a single word for granted. I wanted to get as close as possible to Jesus and was determined to meet him there in the Word. As I pored over the pages, I saw reflected there my own feelings and experiences, and I was assured I need not fear. I would triple-underline, circle, and etch squares around lines with such force that the deep impressions gouged the pages of my Bible—where time and time again I found tangible evidence of hope that, every single time, followed right behind the disappointment.

The Beatitudes promised that suffering is not for nothing, that in my mourning I would be comforted; the psalms of David assured me I am led through the valley of death I was walking; and when all seemed to be lost, Habakkuk promised that my feet would be made like those of a deer and placed on the heights. (See Matthew 5:3–10, Psalm 23, and Habakkuk 3:17–19.) Page after page, line after line, I was assured my Lord God acted on my behalf in real time, and my faith responded in kind.

SEEK AND YOU SHALL FIND

Gone were the days when prayer was confined to the kitchen table at the time when the sun hit the perfect spot in the sky. I had realized that prayer is a posture where I connect with the One who knows me like no other. It is where I find a stillness to lift my praise and offer my pleas; that can be at my kitchen table, on the stoop of the house we would escape to, rocking in the chairs that line my front porch, or sitting cross-legged on the bed in a hotel room.

With steadfast resolve, I had started chasing my Lord God— every day and everywhere. Recording the days and contemplating what I had circled, squared, and underlined in my Bible, I would find him waiting for me, and when I did (and still do), I noted it along with the litany of amens scribbled in my Bible's margins. I was the consummate student in the school of my Jesus, falling in love with whom I was discovering.

But I was also scared—actually, petrified. I was petrified I would miss whatever was to come next. And if that happened, I was sure that would be it. Done. Over. I would be left with a pile of books with scribbled margins and a heart that would once again be smashed and left disappointed and discouraged.

I was desperate not to be passed over. In my mind, the only way to stay in lockstep with the One who had stirred my soul was to smash my nose in his shoulder blade, making it virtually impossible to lose him—and virtually impossible for him to lose *me*. He'd just have to keep tripping over me so that every single time he did, he would know I was still right there.

Then I heard something that would change it all. In just a few simple words from the Gospel of Matthew, I read a promise in scripture that opened my eyes with a tilt-my-head, problem-solved moment: "Ask and it will be given to you; seek and you will find; knock and the door will be opened to you. For everyone who asks, receives; and the one who seeks, finds; and to the one who knocks, the door will be opened" (Mt 7:7–8).

It was so simple: I didn't have to chase him down; I only had to knock. I began to pray these words incessantly. "Here I am, Lord, asking . . . seeking . . . knocking. Let me see the world through your eyes, so I will never be lost." Scrubbing the remnants from dinner's pots, I reclaimed the Lord God: "Give me eyes to see what you want me to see." It was my battle cry, an earnest prayer that I would find the truth I was seeking, as well as the answers to the hard questions I continued to ask.

My sweet friend, prayers prayed with depths of desire will be answered—perhaps not as you envision—but mark my word, they will be answered. My eyes were shown what our Lord God wanted me to see.

SUNDAY SURRENDER

For a long time, one of the few places I cried was in church. I think it is because when I am in church, whether participating in Mass or reflecting in prayer, I feel most at home. I slide into the pew, bow my head, and exhale. I still my soul, ponder the Cross, and am fed—fully and wholly, mind, body, and spirit fed. Participating in Mass was not a *have to* or should do—it was a want to, a yearn to.

But slowly, participating in Mass at the church we belonged, the same one where Catherine had been buried, had become a chore and a challenge. Freddy, Matt, and I would slide into the pew, and I would watch Matt's jaw clench, knowing the announcements would share the latest act of generosity offered on behalf of the "twenty-six," and feel Freddy brace himself in anticipation of my tears, brewing just under the surface.

Homilies would speak to the tragedy and how to forge a path forward. I didn't want to hear about a path forward. I didn't want to hear it, even for just one hour. I just wanted to still my soul and share my heart with my Lord God. So when church became about checking a box and the explanation we offered Freddy as to where are we going was "we have to go to Mass," and my tears were replaced with my bracing, I knew something had to change.

I had heard about a Catholic church in the town next door, and I figured, we might as well give it a try. So one Saturday afternoon, we ducked in through the side door for the Saturday vigil and slid into a side pew. From the moment my knees hit the kneeler, it just felt different; I felt different. The call to worship spoke of the scriptures we would hear and suggested thoughts to ponder, and I bowed low—in this holy and sacred place, we pondered sacred and holy stories.

Gathering his flock in prayer, Fr. Joe sighed and called to a "Dear God" with a love so tender in this holy and sacred place he beckoned my Lord God. The rites and rituals resumed, leading me to the altar and the Eucharist. I was fed, truly satiated, for the first time in what felt like a very long time. I settled back into the pew we had slid into, and a hush fell over the people. In this holy and sacred place I would be fed. And then it happened:

chords from a piano, joined by a sweet and soft voice, drifted over bowed heads, assuring anyone who still wondered that God was in this place.

Tears streamed down my face. I was home.

We found ourselves ducking in through the side door Saturday after Saturday until I finally decided it was not so much where you went to church but where you were fed that was important. I was fed by my Lord God at Sacred Heart Church, so we changed parishes. This simple action fueled and fed my faith at the Saturday vigil week after week. And on Sunday mornings, when the house hummed with a quiet that echoed, the ritual was always the same: me, a cup of coffee, and a sermon series streaming on my laptop straight from a nondenominational church in Atlanta, Georgia. On one Sunday, I can tell you verbatim how it all played out.

In closing, Andy Stanley, the church's pastor, said, "Let me pray for us."

He closed his eyes and tilted his chin toward the heavens. I bowed my head. "Lord God, give me eyes to see what you want me to see . . ."

I lifted my chin, watching in amazement. ". . . and give me ears to hear what you want me to hear, and Father, give me a heart to know your will . . ."

I sighed heavily and closed my eyes, tilted my chin to the heavens, and with praying hands, I gently shook my head and whispered a premature "amen." I awkwardly put my head down—but there was more.

". . . and Father God, grant me the courage to do it. Give me the wisdom to want what you want and the courage to do it. In Jesus' name, amen."

And there it was.

A *knowing* and a *doing*.

So much for smashing my nose in his back and not seeing where I was going. It was time to stop leaning in and to start stepping out. My time of schooling had come to the point where all schooling eventually leads, when it is time to apply all I had learned. It was time to recognize that my fear of being passed over had nothing to do with my Lord God's doing and everything to do with mine. If I wanted to walk in the love I found, I needed to, well, walk. I wasn't sure what I had done in offering a premature amen to something I wasn't 100 percent sure I could deliver, so I wrote it down in my own words to be sure I knew what I was doing.

> Lord God, give me the courage to stop hiding my face. Show me what you want me to see and what you want me to hear. Lord God, stir my soul to do what you want me to do. Lord God, I am afraid. I am afraid I will miss it, afraid that I will mess this all up, afraid that I won't be able to do what you want and that I will let you down, and Lord God, I don't want to disappoint you. Lord God, I don't want to mess this up—oh, please Lord, please make me courageous to do what you want me to do.

In a lot of ways, I think that Sunday morning I surrendered a season I was desperately clinging to—and I hadn't ever really realized it. And maybe my kneejerk response to write it down, to see for myself, was to make sure I wanted to jump from the cliff where I was standing. Done were the days of hiding my face; it was time to see and to hear and to feel for myself.

It boiled down to this: "Lord, I want to want what *you* want me to want." But what was it that he wanted? I pondered that question for a long time, until the answers began to emerge: what he wanted for me—and what he wants for you, my sweet friend—is what he is.

He wants my peace, and he wants your peace—not in a worldly sense where everything falls into place, storms are nothing more than passing showers, and life is an easy, gentle rhythm.

I sigh heavily, thinking about these kinds of pleasant moments. They are great moments. But I do not believe this is the I Am peace that he is. His, I believe, is a deeper stirring of our soul, where it recognizes the divine.

I see my Lord God's hand in the brush strokes of a sunrise, like an oil-painted canvas or color-washed paper or when a block of clay reveals its beautiful form. He is encountered—his peace, revealed—in the way the chords combine into riffs—hands on strings and ebony and ivory keys create a crescendo that reaches the innermost core of my body, igniting every nerve, sending me to a place where—even if I am surrounded by many—space and time are forgotten.

His is the peace that is offered freely and received with eyes that see and ears that hear. But make no mistake, my sweet friend, an oil-covered canvas stashed in an alcove never to be seen with human eyes is a travesty—for the artist and the patron.

His peace is a beautiful exchange that comes with surrendering: surrendering to the notes, allowing them to wash over; and surrendering to the colors of the sunrise, swept across the sky as if from an artist's brush. It's completely counterintuitive—a claiming in the surrendering.

I have such a hard time surrendering, thinking I need whatever I am clinging to. And maybe that is why it was a slow realization. Maybe this is why I had to lean over my kitchen table before I could lean in and step out. And maybe this is why it took some time to pray for eyes that could see. Maybe if I saw what he saw before my heart was made ready, I would have turned back.

When you can see, you realize you're on a journey that seeks to see as Jesus does, and you cannot ignore Calvary.

THE CROSS OF
FORGIVENESS

The Cross is not a comfortable place when you have eyes to see and ears to hear.

It is bearing witness as those who just days before waved palms in the air at his arrival now take up reeds to whip a body raw. Mouths that had sung his praises spit into oozing and open wounds. Having ears to hear the taunting, snickering, and sneering. Hearing the chant of "Crucify him" filling the air, as well as his own excruciating groan, "Forgive them," before he surrendered.

From this vantage point, my prideful shoulders slump in seeing hands that he had held open to the heavens, completely surrendered to his Father's will, now nailed to splintering and knotted wood.

From this perspective, seeing what I see, it should be easy to peel back the fingers of my clenched fists and release everything to which I am holding so tightly. No one was asking me to accept the blunt force of having my hands nailed with iron stakes into a cross, and yet you'd think I was, given how tightly my fists were clenched.

Surrender is hard when fingers are keeping whatever they feel is necessary safe and secure. Have you ever tried to peel back fingers that form squeezed fists? Not easy.

Yet, when you end where the road to Calvary leads and the Cross can't be disregarded, you realize all is surrendered for me and all is surrendered for you so that we are forgiven. You can't ignore what he groans: "Father, forgive them, they know not what they do" (Lk 23:34).

His body freely accepted the blunt-force blows of humanity's sins, and still he utters a prayer on my behalf, on your behalf.

And we know prayers, especially when to our heavenly Father through our Savior, are answered.

There is no other way to his peace. I had prayed for a heart that wants what he wants, and I realized this was a heart that forgives with the same forgiveness he offered then—and offers now.

Forgiveness, in the purest definition, is the release of any debt due. Even when, by human standards, the debt is so egregious, it should be paid in full ten times over, such as the debt owed to a child who is victimized because they trusted the wrong person or to the woman dragged into an alley on her way home from the third shift at a second job. Before Catherine died, I had heard such stories and would shake my head, wondering how forgiveness could be possible in situations like this. I struggled to understand how these people who had been so hurt could stand so strongly and with an overwhelming peace. They seemed to harbor no resentment, nor did they utter a damning word about the assault that left a raw wound and a deep mark.

Before Catherine died, I didn't get it. It seemed to me that if anyone had earned a right to scream their injustice from the mountaintop and claim a debt owed, they did, and yet they didn't. They refused to let their *it* become the all-consuming, defining force of their lives.

And after Catherine died, I found out why: When *it* happens, there is a not-too-subtle temptation to claim a whole lot of "earned" rights—the right to stay in bed, the right to do as you want, and the right to decide who should be held accountable. In the aftermath of the shooting, there seemed to be a race to hold anyone—and everyone—accountable for what had happened, to pay the debt that was owed to us, the families. We were encouraged to join in lashing out at the newspapers, the shooter's family, the school, the community—anybody who could be connected to the pain and hurt that was piling up could be held accountable and owed a debt. The race for accountability and answers exhausted me. So I stepped back and bowed out.

When I stepped back and watched the events unfold, I realized something, something about victims who had suffered before me, the ones I had shaken my head in wonder at how they could harbor no resentment, not utter a damning word: They had walked this journey before me, and the awe I held for them made me think their way was the right way for me. They were not flustered, nor did they exude an anger that felt abrasive and sharp; their gentle faces reflected their sadness and hurt, yet there was peace. It was as if their faces were the face of Jesus.

Maybe they, too, had taken a journey to Calvary; they had seen with eyes to see and heard with ears to hear, and they understood that there are no qualifiers or levels of egregiousness. Maybe they saw what I saw: Jesus does not shift his gaze; despite the egregious injustice he endured, he does not hide his eyes. Maybe they did as Jesus did for them, for me—for you. Maybe they forgave.

This, my beautiful friend, is not easy to do. Think about how hard it is to let it go when your heart is broken into small pieces. It's hard to ignore the hurt in your heart. Believe me, the hurt I was feeling could not be ignored. I warn you though, when you choose to fixate on the hurt, it's hard not to feed it. It could be as simple as being left out. Because you are hurt, you justify hoping that whatever event you were not included in fails miserably or thinking you didn't want to go anyway because it was something so incredibly beneath you. The hurt builds, and then when the person who didn't invite you calls, you are short and they wonder at your abrupt attitude. They think about the conversation, their heart is broken, and the ember that started with your hurt feelings sparks their justification, and all of a sudden there is a full-on wildfire. In reality, the hurt could have been resolved with a simple conversation, an acknowledgment of hurt, and surrender of the pain it created: "I was hurt because . . ." Darkness brought into the light cannot remain dark. It's just not possible.

Please don't think I am being naïve or that I am making it too simple. It is not. Even Jesus, facing the ultimate surrender, "was in such agony and he prayed so fervently that his sweat became like drops of blood falling on the ground" (Lk 22:44). Surrendering debts takes time and does not mean forgetting. Forgetting would return us to where we started, when we had not learned what we now know and with a heart not yet changed—and that would just be insanity and create a never-ending cycle of hurt.

No, forgiveness is releasing another from the debt you feel owed and giving your heart permission to heal instead of keeping score.

The truth is that all debts will be collected one day—not by you and not by me but by the One who settles debts, and in whatever way he deems best. No amount of earthly wealth—material or not—can compensate for the hurt and pain any *it* launches on a heart. Hurt and pain cannot be repaid; they can only be healed.

Perhaps that is why we are told to broadly and swiftly forgive. Maybe forgiving has to do more with us than with whomever we are forgiving. Maybe in offering forgiveness we find a place of peace where our own hearts can heal.

And maybe that's why, when I saw Jesus' Cross with eyes to see as he saw, I saw my heart.

COMING HOME

I drove as the sun rose over the horizon. It had been months since the battle that left my parents and I retreating to our corners of the world and not speaking, a battle that ensued after so much hurt over Catherine's death. Now my father was sick, and his days were numbered. In one sense, I couldn't remember what it was that had divided us, and in another, all I could do was remember for the both of us.

Almost two decades earlier, my father and I had stood at the door of the church on my wedding day. He had looked me square in the eyes, the way I look into Freddy's, and said, "If you have any doubts, we do not need to do this. That car over there—it can take us anywhere." I looked at him with big eyes, and he continued: "And if there is a day in the future, a day that you have doubts, you come home. You can always come home." I shook my head and said OK but that I wanted to do this. And with that, he walked me to the altar and I was married.

After that, life took on a whole new meaning. Fueled by a fast-paced and successful career, I would duck into my parents' house between layovers on business trips, eager to share my latest accomplishments. My mother would look at the two of us, still sitting in front of pushed-back plates from a dinner that had been finished hours before, and comment, "You are your father's daughter."

So when the day came to tell him that I had given up work to stay at home with my children, I was sure he would be truly disappointed. I was the child who had followed in his footsteps into the business world. Now I was turning my back on it. And yet, what I heard was a love powerful and committed: "You are smart, and you know your heart—if this is your heart, you are doing the right thing."

Gradually, the rhythm of life began to shift, and my visits to their house became his surprise drop-ins to mine. Every time Pop pulled into the driveway, my babies would go nuts, the squeal in their voices a dead giveaway as to the identity of the visitor. I felt nostalgic looking on as he spun five-year-old Catherine through the kitchen, just as he had spun me when I was a little girl.

Then came the day when he arrived because my baby girl, his precious granddaughter, had been killed. So absorbed was I in my own grief that I had failed to realize my *it* moment was also his. His and so many others.

It was also a long time before I realized something else: *it* moments that carry the same name do not carry the same response. Grief and suffering are as unique as the lines on our fingertips. While I grieved my baby girl, Freddy grieved his sister, and Matt grieved his daughter. Our parents—her grandparents—were grieving their grandchild, and the list went on and on infinitely. Everyone was facing hurt all their own. It was palpable and proved the saying true: hurt people sometimes hurt people.

REGRET AND
RECRIMINATION

The months and years that followed Catherine's death were filled with the ebb and flow of fresh accusations and reclaimed debts from offenses that should have been forgiven long ago. Hurts that had nothing to do with Catherine's dying came out of left field. Accusations beginning with "I never felt" and "You could have" became barbs that seemed to stab at our wounded hearts, pain oozing from the cracks. And rather than naming it, much like we name storms, the pain of being broken and hurt and scared was named *selfish* and *uncaring*, with lines drawn and months of angry silence.

So now, as I drove to my parents' house, I'd lost count of the days it had been since we had spoken, and I had no idea what I would say when I arrived at their door. My stomach was tight; my hands shook. I was scared and wanted nothing more than to do as Freddy had wanted to do when he was petrified of being rejected from the football team: I wanted to take the next exit, turn around, and go home. But I could not ignore the stirring in my heart that had been nudging me since I had gotten the message my father was dying.

I could easily convince myself that they would never understand and feel justified in keeping the hurt for my own. I could have called them *uncaring* and *insincere* for the way they had treated me. They had never had to break open the frozen earth to bury *their* baby girl—only then could they understand the enormity of what I had endured and see their injustice. Then they would be sorry. I could have kept going, kept feeding the pain.

Of course, this quest for justice was based on a kernel of truth: my family would never understand—could never understand—what I'd been through. But then, neither would I ever understand what *they* were feeling. They had no idea what it was like for me, and I had no idea how it felt for them to stand graveside and watch their baby girl bury hers.

All I knew for certain was I wanted this battle over—all of it. My fighting hands were tired. I wanted to feel some semblance of peace, and in order to find it, I knew my relationship with my parents had to change.

MAKING PEACE

He was in the yard when I pulled up to their house. He looked at me with a faraway look, the question written all over his face: my father was trying to figure out who I was.

The hurt just kept piling on. I had waited too long. I should have listened to the stirring months ago. I should have come right away when the swords were first drawn and said, *Let's not do this.*

And now the days he could remember were even fewer than I realized.

I braced myself and got out of the car. Looking at him, I whispered, "Dad," and somehow he realized it was me.

"Jenny," he said, half as a question and half in confirmation that it was in fact me. I looked at him through pooling eyes and nodded.

His expression lifted. It was as if he was expecting me. "You're home. Come in."

Truth is, I wasn't sure I could. My clenched fingers were digging craters into my palms, and my feet felt as if they had melted into the cement curb. He put his hand on the small of my back and spoke as if he remembered similar words he had said on my wedding day: "Let's go."

The door opened and before I knew what to say, I blurted out, "I am done with this—I cannot fight anymore." And with that, clenched fists released and a hand that had forgotten what it felt like to be open surrendered to the heavens a lifetime of my own expectations of my parents. Everything changed that day. And it changed not because of what my parents said or did but because I had changed.

It was the first step in a knowing I was changed.

Our relationship would not go back to the place it was before Catherine died. It can't, and it shouldn't. If it did, we would be right back to where we started, not having learned, loved, or grown—all that hurt would go right back to where it was with the yoke of Catherine's death.

And claiming the yoke is not easy.

CLAIMING THE YOKE

That yoke was not light, and the burden was not an easy one. The passage from Matthew seemed like some cruel joke: "Come to me, all you who labor and are burdened, and I will give you rest. . . . For my yoke is easy, and my burden light" (Mt 11:28, 30).

Easy? Light? I was stumbling and tripping and falling all over the pain and frustration that littered my path: Catherine's death, the fallout with family, a marriage that had gone from faltering to shattered, and now my father's illness.

When a new struggle surfaced, I had to go through the process of dealing with it. I had become very comfortable shaking my fists at my Lord God, accusing him of not keeping his promise to love me. I would challenge him, letting him know I found fault with his word choice. His yoke was not light, and the burden had hardly been easy. I would remind him that he could have done something to lessen my load or at least keep the struggle at bay until the one I was wrestling was over. But he didn't, so clearly, as he didn't make the way easy and light, he didn't love me.

But wait. There I was, praying to my Lord God, asking for a heart that mirrored his. And somewhere along the way, I had decided his should reflect mine. Suddenly the scripture that I claimed as my creed didn't seem so relevant.

> For though the fig tree does not blossom,
>   and no fruit appears on the vine,
> Though the yield of the olive fails
>   and the terraces produce no nourishment,
> Though the flocks disappear from the fold
>   and there is no herd in the stalls,
> Yet I will rejoice in the LORD
>   and exult in my saving God.
> GOD, my Lord, is my strength;
>   he makes my feet swift as those of deer
>   and enables me to tread upon the heights. (Hb
>   3:17–19)

The heights I was being taken to were not what I envisioned, so I was trying to force my will upon God, demanding that he restore to me every bit of what had been lost: I had lost love, so I wanted more. I felt lonely, so I wanted a friend. Somewhere along the way, only a tit-for-tat ransom, I had decided, would restore my faith and justify the pain he had allowed to touch my life. When the ransom went unpaid, my frustration escalated and the more I felt my Lord God owed me.

It had become a vicious cycle. I was hiding behind the cloak of what I thought I had earned and what was proper payment, and I would launch demands. Then I'd in some way be convicted and see him with the eyes I had prayed for. I saw a Father slow to anger, patient, and kind, and I would be reminded of the blessings he had poured over me. I would fall to my knees, pleading and claiming the forgiveness offered on the Cross. "Father, forgive me; I know not what I do."

And because our Father is slow to anger, patient, and kind, I would be forgiven. Seven times seven hundred seventy-seven times, I would be forgiven, and every single time, I would chastise myself. I felt worthless, and this was pointless because I was undeserving. I felt I had come this far and was wholly inadequate to continue. In one fell swoop of my worthlessness pity party, I denied the very thing for which he bled, hanging from the Cross: his love for me.

Over and over again, when what I wanted did not play out in my time and in my way, I would launch heartbreak over the bow, claiming I had endured enough and now it was my turn and my time to be *happy*.

I was hiding behind an unspoken expectation that my heavenly Father should make me *happy*. He should have shielded me from the pain I had endured, not only when Catherine died but also before and after she died. If he loved me, he would not expose me to such pain, or at least he would acknowledge and reward my faithful response. But I felt he didn't, and now, in my opinion, he owed me.

He didn't stop the pain I had endured in my life. He didn't stop the shooter who walked into Catherine's classroom and took her life. He didn't stop the disease that was claiming my father's brain. And he wasn't doing anything to spare me from what had become the heated battle of a contentious divorce that would threaten to suck what life I had left. Pain upon pain just kept piling on, putting all sorts of pressure on a heavy heart that had started keeping count of the debt I felt God owed to me.

I had slid into making a bold and dangerous assumption, creating a kind of quid pro quo relationship with my Lord God that would never, could never, satisfy because it was not based on the truth: that the heart of my Lord God seeks mine and claims mine for no other reason than he loves me. His is a covenant heart that gives freely and lavishly and will not be made to deliver anything less than what is for his child's very best. He will never deliver on my wants when those wants are not for my very best; sometimes it is in the breaking that we are made better.

I wish I could tell you the exact moment I realized what was happening, but I can't; there was no epiphany—just a slow awakening. When I realized the game I was playing, it crushed me.

With every fiber of my being I dug deep and bowed low and surrendered it all, releasing every claim I had made.

> Lord God, I know you can stop a tragic and sudden death, and you allowed Catherine's. Father God, I surrender to your way and know you know best.
>
> Lord God, I know you bring sight to the blind and hearing to the deaf, and you did not offer this miraculous healing to my father. Abba Father, I surrender to and accept your will.
>
> Lord God, you restore relationships, singing redemption's songs, and yet you do not sing over my failed marriage. Father God, I trust in your unfailing love and that you will bring beauty from these ashes.
>
> Lord God, Abba Father, I will wait on you. Forgive me, Father, for I do not know what I do.

I was no longer hiding behind what I felt due for the tragedy and hurt I had experienced. Rather, my gaze was now focused on him with a heart just beginning to understand. His are the eyes that look at me gently, acknowledging the pain and suffering and asking for nothing; there are no debts for me to pay or ransom to return. His heart looks at me with a love so great, and this I know is true: he wants me to offer his heart to those around me, a heart that bears no grudge, holds no ransom, and claims no debt. It is a heart that acknowledges, in all that is painful and all that hurts, him and the beauty he is bringing from the ashes. For this I know . . .

> Yet I will rejoice in the LORD
> and exult in my saving God. (Hb 3:18)

Circled, squared, and triple-underlined is the simple fact that despite the pain, there is goodness for no other reason than he is. And he will.

You see, my prayer to see, to hear, and to mirror was answered and continues to be answered. In surrendering the pain and the struggles that hurt and giving up my claim for debts, I am given peace. And in that peace I see: He is peace. He is love. He is forgiveness, offered and received.

Forgiveness is where we are changed, both in forgiving those who have launched assaults and in forgiving ourselves. Peace is where we discover how to release that which weighs us down, so we are equipped to continue on this journey with our Lord God, where our feet are made swift like a deer's to tread upon the heights.

find your sanctuary

Rescue me from violent bloodshed, God,
my saving God,
and my tongue will sing joyfully of your
justice.
Lord, you will open my lips;
and my mouth will proclaim your praise.
For you do not desire sacrifice or I would
give it;
a burnt offering you would not accept.
My sacrifice, O God, is a contrite spirit;
a contrite, humbled heart, O God, you
will not scorn.
—Psalm 51:16–19

1. "Grief and suffering are as unique as the lines on our fingertips." How might the same be true of forgiveness? What is God asking you to surrender?

2. In his parable about the unforgiving servant (see Matthew 18:21–35), Jesus speaks of a man who refused to forgive a debt much smaller than his own. Is forgiveness a necessary part of redemptive suffering? Why or why not?

3. God will use all pain and suffering for his good and his purpose, and sometimes, pain and suffering seem relentless. Does this resonate with your experiences? How did you respond?

CHAPTER 8

a kingdom
of peace

At thirtysomething, I thought I knew it all. I was oh so wise and knowing. I couldn't understand why the mama whose baby just dripped off her would offer a tired smile and raise her eyebrows as if saying to me, "What can you do?" My put-together, wise childless self would smile back a cordial smile and think, *A lot.*

I had the impression that raising children was the same as tackling a project at work. By digging deep and embracing a few late nights in the office, in a matter of time, you send them off and toast a job well done. Any mama would chuckle silently at my naïve analogy and offer a skeptically kind "OK" and smile her Mona Lisa smile when I asserted that *my* babies—the ones I had not yet labored into the world—would be picture perfect in every way, astute and cultured and perfectly put together.

As I said, I thought I was wise and knowing. It all seemed so simple.

And it *is* simple . . . until midnights in a creaky rocker leave you praying the fever will break and allow baby to sleep. And when it doesn't, the panic builds as you realize that in a matter of hours, the two-year-old sleeping on the other side of the wall will be awake and you may very well still be sitting on this rocker.

Did I replace the bottle of juice in the fridge after he finished the last one yesterday? you wonder idly. Suddenly life isn't so perfectly put together. With one restless baby clinging to your sweat-soaked nightgown and another fussy from hearing there is no juice, you realize what that mama's raised eyebrows and Mona Lisa smile really meant.

Simple all of a sudden is a complicated and delicate dance with the tiny souls that you labored out and over. Yes, my thirtysomething self was so unknowing. And you know what? I am grateful she was, because otherwise I may not have bought that piece of art.

PICTURE PERFECT

Almost as soon as I knew I was going to become a mother, I had decided the baby in my rounding belly would have an appreciation for the arts. The crescendo of an orchestra would bring him to tears, and together we would stand mesmerized in front of canvases in the galleries we would visit. I believed then, as I do now, that the very heart and the very soul of humanity are presented through our creativity: the characters in our books, the chords and lyrics of our music, and the colors splayed on our canvases. Creativity is a sacred gift, an expression of our being made in the image of the divine, and I thought an infant should know this from the outset.

And because of this, I refused to hang any of the accoutrements the magazines and catalogs assured were the perfect pairing to baby's first nursery. Nope, not on my watch. I had decided the walls of his nursery should reflect the galleries we would someday visit.

So I decided to buy a print of a classic work of art for Freddy. It was a big deal, this piece of art. I laugh at the thought now—I really believed this one piece would make or break the character of the baby in my belly. I actually lost sleep over what the image should be.

And maybe I lost sleep because it was a big deal. Because it was a big deal, just not in the way I had thought it was. I should have just settled my restless soul and trusted that I would find the right print. But that would be placing trust in God, and my thirtysomething, not-so-wise self had a very different relationship with God.

And after sleepless nights, I landed on what it would be: Edward Hicks's *The Peaceable Kingdom* (ca. 1834), a masterpiece about the animals of the wild joining forces with a child. Lions, lambs, calf, wolves, and an angelic child was the perfectly appointed masterpiece to complete the perfectly appointed nursery welcoming my newborn home.

For seven years, I committed every detail of that image to memory, in the same way I had when I studied the masters' canvases. I pondered the image from the well-worn rocker and eventually a far-too-narrow bed, searching every single detail, every character—for hours.

It was here in the small nursery that we learned to decompress; you could say it was our sanctuary. We'd flop into the creaky rocking chair, and his head would rest upon my beating heart. Eventually he'd sigh, and I knew he finally slept. With my chin resting on his head, our hearts beating in unison to the whir of the rocker, stillness settled, and I would study each animal and the small child that seemed to be waving to me from this place where lambs rested with lions.

In time the nursery became Catherine's, and in the darkness of night, a small light casting a glow across the frame, I would chase the words around the perimeter of the image, wondering how closely it reflected the truth. "Then the wolf shall be a guest of the lamb, and the leopard shall lie down with the young goat; The calf and the young lion shall browse together, with a little child to guide them" (Is 11:6).

For seven years, every detail seared and branded my mind and would later assure me I had not missed the miracle.

MOVING ON

Months before Catherine died, we moved across town, having outgrown the little house that welcomed us to Newtown, Connecticut. The kids needed space, we needed space, and well, life was changing, and we needed change.

We had decided on a house that would allow my babies to return to their friends at Sandy Hook Elementary in the fall, and they were ecstatic. It was now safe for them to go beyond the driveway; we were surrounded by neighbors—neighbors with kids and a teenage girl Catherine wished aloud was her sister, leaving a love note in the girl's mailbox.

You can imagine what those neighbors might have thought though when, on the first day we were in the house, at a not so neighborly hour, my babies took to circling the cul-de-sac on their scooter and bike, Catherine's nightgown billowing behind her. It was our grand entrance. If there were a moment when the saying Life is Good described a good life, this was it.

Catherine died four months later. It was within the confines of that home that I would be forced to cobble together the words and complete the sentence every obituary contains. I was stuck. What do you put at the end of a sentence that starts with "In lieu of flowers, the family is requesting . . ."?

What I wanted to write was, "In lieu of flowers, I'd like my baby girl back," but that wasn't something that any cause or initiative could offer in return for the donations it received marked with the note "in memory of Catherine."

I was stuck on what would be Catherine's cause, because that was the way that sentence was supposed to end. I never considered what Catherine's cause, agenda, or initiative would be, and why would I? She was six.

Truth is, though, she had one. Every six-year-old has a cause, and it's pretty simple to discover. Six-year-olds live in the present with hearts fully exposed, and they scream about what delights them. Take a glimpse at what they are drawing, writing, and singing about, and it's pretty clear. Watch as they set up their pretend worlds on the floor and play out imaginary scenes. There is no mistaking. Where you find a six-year-old's heart is where you find their cause.

Catherine's heart was animals—all the animals. She created imaginary shelters and farms. Her little hands tucked the little animals into paddocks and completed the exams that would make them better. She wrote books about "hauses" (horses) and drew pictures of all the animals in her care.

She would care for them all, she promised. Every last one of them.

That memory inspired me to write what I knew would support her cause: "In lieu of flowers, the family is requesting donations be made to the Animal Center of Newtown." We knew that the only way to honor Catherine was to honor the animals she adored, and the animal control center, "the pound," made sense. But in the fog of planning and the rush of just getting the words on paper, we failed to include one simple word: "control."

They say God writes straight with crooked lines. And sometimes he works in the gaps. As we were soon to find out, that little word—"control"—made all the difference. When we left out *control*, we made way for a miracle.

And so, as donation envelopes poured in from all over the world, they did not go to the Animal Control Center as we thought; they went instead to the Animal Center, a small, all-volunteer, local, nonprofit animal rescue organization. My omission set into motion what would become the place where I would find that sanctuary I'd been seeking all along.

A GRACE-FILLED MISTAKE

Three weeks after Catherine died, the women from the Animal Center sat across the table, warming their hands around steaming coffee cups, their swollen and tired eyes pooled to overflowing as we shared stories of Catherine's gentle spirit. It was clear to me that these were her kindred spirits: they, too, loved animals and made a commitment to care for them.

They had received donations on Catherine's behalf from across the globe. Letters with checks from mamas who couldn't imagine losing their own precious children and crumpled dollar bills from kids who wrote, "For Catherine." Broken hearts sent what they could, hoping to start something that would heal mine.

There at our kitchen table, our new friends from the Animal Center asked if we had thoughts about the best way to use the donations they had received—more than $100,000 in donations so far, with more still coming. With a simple slip of my pen, these women now faced what seemed an insurmountable task: not simply finding homes for a few cats and dogs but finding a way to honor a little girl they had never met. It was a journey we would embark upon together—one they had not anticipated. With kind and gentle swollen eyes, they shared what they thought might be a way to honor Catherine.

I sat transfixed as they described their vision: a place where a child, looking into the eyes of a lamb, dog, or kitten, would know their innate beauty; the animal, looking back, would know safety and human compassion. It would be a place of healing, a sanctuary in the truest sense.

As they spoke, I looked again at that picture that had hung in the nursery and now hung behind them: the lamb lying with the lion and a little child inviting me in—the perfectly appointed masterpiece I had painstakingly chosen before either of my babies was born. When we moved, I had decided to hang *The Peaceable Kingdom* in my dining room. And then, at that moment, I realized it was a sign.

I looked into their eyes and answered, "Yes, this is what we will do."

WHISPERS OF DOUBT

In the years that followed my fiat, I poured myself into the place that would honor Catherine. The bus stop, prayer, my work for the sanctuary, and back to the bus stop was the routine that defined the rhythm of my days. It was a quiet undertaking that at times overwhelmed me and at others left me in a puddle of doubt. But I could not give up, not for anything. I kept searching for a location that would work for Catherine's sanctuary, people to help with the sanctuary, and answers for what to do when I found them.

There were so many questions. I had questions, and the people I was meeting had questions. I had gotten good at anticipating what they would ask. Just as people used to question me in the grocery store, I was getting stopped again—only now the questions were "Tell me, what was she like? Tell me, what is this sanctuary that you are building? Tell me, how are you?" And often they would not understand the answers I gave. They would nod politely, offer their sincerest condolences, and wish me the very best.

At times exhaustion tipped the scale far enough for doubt to scurry in and whisper deflating thoughts: *Well, she was only six. You are insane to think that this is something that would honor her heart. This was far too big an aspiration.*

And really, what about Freddy? Doubt would continue, taking a different tack. *What was my work with the sanctuary doing to Freddy? He is the only one you have left, and you should pour into him the way you are pouring into her—she doesn't need you; he does.*

Doubt was working hard to convince my heart that Catherine's dying had released me from any claim of being her mama. But I recognized immediately the lies. Big fat lies. I am a mama of *two* children, one of whom is in heaven and one who continues to walk this earth.

It was heartbreaking and confusing, and I was wrestling with what I was hearing, all the while wrestling with my Lord God. I was looking for any kind of answers and assurance. You probably know what I am going to say: a seeking heart will find.

UPSIDE-DOWN MOMENTS

Word had spread that we had decided to build a sanctuary in Catherine's honor, and the offers to help gained traction. One of the offers was from the family of Newtown-based P|H Architects. They had come to our home with a simple offer: whatever they could do, they would.

And help they would. In the months that followed I met the architects at property after property. Hours upon hours we would walk the perimeters of various properties, and they would explain and describe and point out the possibilities and warn about the pitfalls. Inevitably the pitfalls would prevail, and the possibilities would fall flat. Finally I saw the right place—and knew it immediately.

At this property, we walked a violet-covered trail with tall meadow grasses bending in the wind. Our guide, the deputy director of Land Use and Planning, told us they didn't hay the fields until the fall because "in the meadows is where the mama deer hide their babies." He had no idea what he had just said. Catherine collected mamas and babies. She would line them up, mama and baby, side by side.

And just like that, I knew this was the place. Yes, this was the place where my heart would find my baby.

Less than a month later, I pulled my chair up to the long table in the architects' office, exchanging lighthearted banter before getting down to business. The banter quickly faded into the background when I heard Jack Johnson's "Upside Down"—Catherine's favorite—playing softly in the background, riveting my attention. At that moment, the talking became background noise as I was taken back to watching *Curious George* with Catherine, cozied up on the couch together. Catherine was a movie girl, and as the credits rolled and that song played, she had begged and pleaded for a monkey just like George. And now the song was playing again in their office.

As the last line of the song faded, the irony of the lyrics about finding things that can't be found and sharing love washed over me. Here we were, talking about how to honor my baby girl buried six months before. Little did I realize, Jack Johnson had it all figured out.

Moments later, the reason for my being in their office was revealed. They turned back an oversized page, and I took in my breath sharply, enchanted. It was exquisite. I was shown on paper what they had explained with arms flying and hands pointing out every "You could" and "This would be" as we walked the property. I didn't think it was possible to make the place we had found more beautiful than the day I walked around it with them—the day I noticed grace in the way grasses do not fight but lean into the breeze. But they had.

I stared at the paper as if it were a master's canvas on a gallery wall. I pored over every detail as they went back and forth, describing the meaning and intention behind each water-colored structure—the vision of the sanctuary we would build. I could not look away. In one corner was their name, their stamp of commitment to this place of healing: P|H Architects had taken the sanctuary on as a pro bono client.

What they did not know is that this place of healing for humans and animals alike we were committed to building had started right then and there.

Since Catherine had died, I felt painfully alone, and my world had become painfully upside down, with darkness threatening to encroach. Doubt was doing its best to establish a stronghold. But on that day, there was a changing of the guard, and hope took its rightful and true place in the kingdom. On that day, my hope was restored in the very place where my healing would be found: a sanctuary in the truest and purest sense.

AWAKENINGS

The land was gifted, and the work began. Vines that had twisted and choked for years were pulled back and cleared, making way for a beautiful transformation. Other people joined us to help, and over time, laughter floated on the gentle breeze that bent the grasses and peace emerged as the sunsets painted the sky every color imaginable.

Once we were finished, horses galloped across the trails, and dogs and cats with soulful eyes found their forever homes. No longer fawns, the deer would come out from hiding and meander in front of us and the butterflies. I hope someday you see them. The butterflies swarm. They had emerged just as the sanctuary had; it was a beautiful awakening.

I brought two children into this world; one still hops on the bus, and the other shows herself in all that is the sanctuary. Although Catherine no longer graces the earth, I am still her mother, and I still have feelings of responsibility toward her and everything she held dear.

As I work on behalf of the sanctuary, I often encounter Catherine in the people who come alongside me to help. Their fierce determination reminds me of the day that Catherine dug in, to the point of frustrated tears, to be able to show her brother that she could ride her bike without training wheels. I see her persistence in how so many people have gathered around, working and reworking to overcome every obstacle; these people, I still say, are gifts from Catherine.

There are so many who offered their gifts—talents poured out from every direction as people came together to do what they could to realize this place for Catherine. They would not judge and wonder, as I was afraid they would. They were kind, even those who were painfully out of place and awkward—just as I often felt. Encounters with them reminded me of something Catherine used to say: "Oh, but they were *kind*." And so, these ones who accept me for my painfully awkward self—and who still offer what they can give—they, too, are gifts from Catherine.

Everywhere I look, I see her: The faces that light up when an insect is placed in their palm. Arms wrapped around necks, drawing animals close as, nose to nose, they connect with a puppy or kitten. And every so often, I overhear the small, whispered promise of my daughter's voice, assuring that she would take care of them. Young and old, the compassionate souls who also promise to care for the animals are gifts from Catherine.

The gifts abound, and I mark down the days, thanking my Lord God for this place where he brought me. And yet still there are days that I wonder, *Could this be from you, Lord God?* Could it be that I am loved in such a way that I sigh deeply in the knowledge that I have found a love that settles my restless soul and soothes my broken heart?

I still sometimes hear that almost imperceptible whisper that causes the smallest seed of doubt to take root.

But time passes, and I am stronger now. It doesn't stay rooted for long.

BUILDING THE WALL

With boulders and carefully chiseled stone covering the small space, we had begun the first phase for the water-colored buildings on the architect's plans I had cried over six years before. To anyone else, the work we were doing could hardly be considered exciting: dirt, drainage, and a retaining wall that keeps it all together. Anyone else who would think this had it all wrong. My Lord God was in the midst of what was to become an unfolding, making everything upside down and mirror image from how it should be, and this was just the beginning—the first fruits of what was to come.

Piece by piece, the retaining wall was stacked. Day by day, the stones were chiseled and purposefully arranged. Then I received a call: "The master stonemason had a thought and would like to incorporate it into the wall."

The thought was far more than a "thought."

He had been sitting in a pew, offering his own goodbye to his own loved one, when he had the thought. He leaned over to his wife and asked for a pen to capture his idea. He had his own way of recording the days—he drew them.

The image that emerged from the stonemason's drawing was both sacred and divine, and he was hoping to include it in the wall he was stacking.

There would be a single massive boulder that was the earth on which a sun shone over. Reaching from the sun were rays that, as he said, were reaching to us from heaven. The picture he drew would be revealed in the stone chiseled and stacked on top of raw rock in just the spot where the sun reaches down into the sanctuary every morning.

When I stand and ponder the masterpiece in front of me, I wonder, *Is it as he said, or is it as I felt?* He told me that as he sat in the pew, drawing his idea, he realized it was as if heaven was reaching down to earth in an assurance that, *yes, Catherine is there.*

Yes, she is there, and my Lord God is here. The sun's rays reminded me of the rays of sun that covered my table as I sat in the days after Catherine died, rays that flood the sky as the storm clouds break. Yes, surely heaven does reach down to earth.

Yet, it could also be turned upside down. The image carved and stacked in rock could also be my arms stretching to the heavens, offering a plea to my Lord God to lift me into his arms—arms lifted in knowing and trusting his promise is true—he is always right there.

Here in this place I call sanctuary, where heaven and earth collide, I have discovered sanctuary is not a place but a state of being. It is where the gentle breezes that bend the grasses reveal what my heart has discovered as truth.

Sanctuary is a place of healing where all that has broken is tended and the soothing balm of love is gently applied. And sanctuary is a safe haven, a place of peace that knows all the ways my heart has been made to understand, even in the breaking and the beating, that it is covered in a love far greater than I will ever understand.

You know, storms will always threaten, and at times the clouds will converge and my heart will be broken. And when that happens, I no longer cower and hide but trust in the restoration that will follow.

All that is asked of me is that, like the grasses that wave in the breezes at the sanctuary, I lean into the One whose breath breathed the breeze, trusting beyond anything that I may understand, that I will be restored with a heart more beautiful and stronger than I could imagine.

Sanctuary is my heart where his kingdom has been restored.

find your sanctuary

For though the fig tree does not blossom,
    and no fruit appears on the vine,
Though the yield of the olive fails
    and the terraces produce no nourishment,
Though the flocks disappear from the fold
    and there is no herd in the stalls,
Yet I will rejoice in the Lord
    and exult in my saving God.

> GOD, my Lord, is my strength;
>> he makes my feet swift as those of deer
>> and enables me to tread upon the
>> heights.
>
> —Habakkuk 3:17–19 (emphasis added)

1. Habakkuk is my creed, an assurance of the voice of my Lord God's provision and love. What scripture verses would you call your creed?
2. How would you describe the place where you find peace, your sanctuary?
3. Consider the suffering in your own life. What has been the reward?

conclusion

In my favorite picture of the two of us, Catherine's head fits perfectly into the space between my shoulder and neck. I know the exact moment it was taken, at a Thanksgiving parade, but I barely recognize myself. There are times I've wondered, had she survived, would I be the person in that picture today? Would I have been awoken to the love that lifts my eyes to the morning sun and dries my tears? Had she survived, would I plead with God to mold me into the person he created or be afraid I will somehow stray from the path that leads to him? Would I have wondered whether I was worthy?

My journey answered these questions in such a way as I will never need to utter such questions again.

Our Lord God is relentless in his love and does not waver in drawing his children to his heart. I am his child, and he will not waver. Never. Whether through Catherine's death or trials since or through the joys I have experienced and the graces I have been afforded, I have been changed and transformed—I would not be who I am today if I had not walked through them.

In the years since December 14, 2012, I have grieved a marriage that did not survive the shattering blows of Catherine's death. And as if that was not enough, while in the throes of divorce's heated battle, I buried both my father and my grandmother within six months of each other. Clearly, there is no check box for suffering.

In the exhaustion of grieving, energy used on keeping secrets and feelings stuffed in the crevices of my heart was depleted, and the cover that was keeping everything tucked securely in place was lifted. That which I thought long gone or dealt with, over years surfaced and joined the choir of the grief I was feeling.

The saying is true: grief begets grief in the same way that hurt begets hurt. There had been so much stuffed away when it came to my marriage. I think my dad knew this when he gave me an out at the church on my wedding day. But then again, everything seems so much clearer in the rearview mirror. Catherine's death unearthed all that I had been holding onto. And when it bubbled to the surface, it sent not only my marriage spiraling but also my family and friends scattering.

On the battlefield of divorce, my newfound faith was tested. On days I felt left with no defenses, I would retreat to the Word and was quickly reminded that a battle fought well is a battle fought from bended knees. The testing proved that what is forged in the fire is made stronger and more beautiful. I am ashamed I carry the title "divorced." It is not a badge I want, but I know that because of it, I am changed and transformed for the better.

My divorce was chaotic and toxic and lonely and quiet; it rattled not only me but also Freddy. Pain once again piled on top of pain, and I found myself looking him square in the eyes and assuring him I would be fine, he would be fine—that we would be just fine. *Fine*, though, is defined far differently than what it once was.

You see, in this time and the suffering it brought, I did not blindly accept and painfully pretend I was OK and put together. I leaned in and pressed forward and did not hide my fears. I spoke them into the light. True and authentic to the heart that had been transformed in the years since Catherine's death, I accepted help and shared my heart fully and completely. Places I had kept in the dark were exposed to the light, and the hurts I had spent years rationalizing were soothed in the love I had come to find in my Lord God. My Bible's margins are marred with my pleas, and the days written in my journal are dark and frantic: reminders are darkest before the dawn. And whether I believed it or not at the time, there is a dawn and it comes every morning.

I have also realized in the years since December 14, 2012, joy is not something manufactured, and blessings, whether I deem myself worthy or not, will be bestowed. I have found myself lingering long at the table as Freddy shares the stories of his days. It is here that I witness the spark in his eye and know that God is assuring me my son, my Brave One, while nicked up in the fight, will be fine.

And I have stopped—stopped striving and stopped trying to do it all on my own—because you see, it is in the hands that have taken mine that I am reminded I do not walk alone and that I will never walk alone.

And I am quick to seek forgiveness and plead for a heart that forgives—no longer do I feed the fire of entitlement and embarrassment. I have found that a heart that does not carry judgment is a heart that can climb heights unknown. I protect that heart, my heart, at all costs.

In the days that have become years since December 14, 2012, I have been made ready for my journey to come. The faith I found in the days of Catherine's death equipped me for the days that marked my marriage's end. And the faith that grew in the days of grieving my marriage I am sure has readied my heart for storms surely gathering on the horizon.

My dear friend, please don't wince in thinking, *Hasn't she suffered enough?* It is because of the storms that I have found the peace with which I am sustained.

Storms will gather, and when they do, I will be sheltered in the peace of my Lord God. And in that knowing, I can embrace the here and now, the joys and challenges of today, and today alone, knowing they are preparing me for whatever tomorrow may bring. And in that knowing, I am blessed. Blessed abundantly.

Jennifer Hubbard is the president and executive director of the Catherine Violet Hubbard Animal Sanctuary, which she founded in memory of her daughter who died in the Sandy Hook Elementary School shooting. Hubbard is a national Catholic speaker and retreat leader and is frequently featured at Legatus gatherings. She also is an award-winning writer with *Magnificat*.

She has been a guest on a variety of national television shows, including *Today*, *CBS News*, and *ABC News*. She also has been featured on Catholic News Agency and is a monthly guest on *Spirit Morning Radio* in Omaha, Nebraska.

Hubbard earned her bachelor's degree from Randolph Macon Women's College. She is a member of the board of trustees at Fraser Woods Montessori School. She lives with her son in Sandy Hook, Connecticut.

CVHFoundation.org
Facebook: Jennifer Sullivan Hubbard
Instagram: Jenshubb

Fr. Peter Cameron, O.P., director of formation and ecclesiastical liaison for Hard as Nails Ministry, was the founding editor-in-chief of *Magnificat*.

AVE

AVE MARIA PRESS

Founded in 1865, Ave Maria Press,
a ministry of the Congregation of
Holy Cross, is a Catholic publishing
company that serves the spiritual and
formative needs of the Church and its
schools, institutions, and ministers;
Christian individuals and families; and
others seeking spiritual nourishment.

For a complete listing of titles from

Ave Maria Press

Sorin Books

Forest of Peace

Christian Classics

visit www.avemariapress.com